Loving on Me!

Lessons Learned on the Journey from MESS to MESSAGE

KATRINA McGHEE

BALBOA.
PRESS

A DIVISION OF HAY HOUSE

Balboa Press books may be ordered through booksellers or by contacting:

Balboa Press
A Division of Hay House
1663 Liberty Drive
Bloomington, IN 47403
www.balboapress.com
1 (877) 407-4847

Because of the dynamic nature of the Internet, any web addresses or links contained in this book may have changed since publication and may no longer be valid. The views expressed in this work are solely those of the author and do not necessarily reflect the views of the publisher, and the publisher hereby disclaims any responsibility for them.

The author of this book does not dispense medical advice or prescribe the use of any technique as a form of treatment for physical, emotional, or medical problems without the advice of a physician, either directly or indirectly. The intent of the author is only to offer information of a general nature to help you in your quest for emotional and spiritual well-being. In the event you use any of the information in this book for yourself, which is your constitutional right, the author and the publisher assume no responsibility for your actions.

Any people depicted in stock imagery provided by Thinkstock are models, and such images are being used for illustrative purposes only. Certain stock imagery © Thinkstock.

All Scripture quotations, unless otherwise indicated, are taken from the *New Living Translation Holy Bible*. (NLT) New Living Translation Copyright© 1996, 2004, 2007, 2013 by Tyndale House Foundation.

Scripture quotation marked (NASB) is taken from the *New American Standard Bible*. Copyright © 1960, 1962, 1963, 1968, 1971, 1972, 1973, 1975, 1977, 1995 by The Lockman Foundation.

Scripture quotation marked (NIV) is taken from the *Holy Bible, New International Version*®, NIV® Copyright ©1973, 1978, 1984, 2011 by Biblica, Inc.®

Scripture quotation marked (KJV) is taken from the *King James Version*.

Scripture quotation marked (BSB) is taken from the *Berean Study Bible*. © 2015 by Bible Hub and Berean Bible.

All scripture quotations marked (NKJV) are taken from the *New King James Version*®. Copyright © 1982 by Thomas Nelson.

Print information available on the last page.

ISBN: 978-1-5043-4929-1 (sc)
ISBN: 978-1-5043-4931-4 (hc)
ISBN: 978-1-5043-4930-7 (e)

Library of Congress Control Number: 2016901003

Balboa Press rev. date: 02/10/2016

For God, who healed my body, restored my soul,
and filled me with love, overflowing.

THANKS AND LOVE

They say it takes a village to raise a child, but I'm convinced as adults we need our own tribe too—a group of people who are willing to tell us the truth in love, and then despite our errant ways, love us anyhow. I am so grateful to God for the amazing souls He has placed in mine. Without them this book, and this amazing journey, would not have been possible.

To my parents, Frank, Jr. and Patricia McGhee, thanks for your cheers, corrections, compassion, and love. You are my heroes.

To my son Brandon, thanks for believing in my dreams and encouraging me to do the same. You are my heart.

To my brother Frank, sister-in-love Tomiko, and my niece Chelsea, thanks for always being there. I can always count on you.

To my cousin Tanya, thanks for your hugs that helped me heal, and for your infectious joy that restored my smile. You are my sister in spirit.

To my kindred spirit Groesbeck, thank you for reminding me that I am enough and never letting me forget. You are my truth-teller and sage.

To my mentor Hattie and my transition coach Debi, thank you for "shining the light" while I did the work. You are my guides.

To my pastor, Dr. Frederick D. Haynes, III, thank you for always praying for me, before I could even ask. You are my beloved shepherd.

To my friends Andrea, Carlie, Carol, Cheryl, Crystal, Erica, Gina, Janet, Kenna, Larry, Sybil, Terri and Torie—thanks for your encouragement and support. You inspire me to soar.

To my fellow Loving on Me writers, thank you for helping bring this vision to fruition. You are changing the world, one soul at a time.

… And to my doggy, Romulus, thanks for being the best writing companion a girl could ever have. You make me smile, every day. ❧

CONTENTS

INTRODUCTION

Oh God ... I'm having a heart attack and stroke at the same time. Chest tight and face numb, I could barely take a breath.

Crap! I'm 44 years old, and stress is killing me. Waiting to see the doctor, I closed my eyes and prayed I would be okay.

How did I let my dream job turn my life into such a nightmare? When I get out of here, I need to make some changes—and fast!

Isn't it crazy how life can change in the blink of an eye? One day we're cruising along just fine, and the next we run smack dab into the middle of a "life-interrupted" moment—an experience so significant it completely transforms our perspective and priorities.

For some of us it's a traumatic event such as a divorce, illness, or unexpected job change. For others it's an encounter with an idea or person who dramatically challenges our thinking, causing us to question the paradigms that have previously shaped our perspectives. Whichever the case may be, life-interrupted moments are game changers. We can't always articulate what's different, but we know beyond a shadow of a doubt there has to be more than what we've known before.

I was there just a few short years ago, when a professional calamity turned into a personal crisis. In the blink of an eye I went from a life I loved, full of purpose and meaning, to being unemployed, sick from anxiety and exhaustion, and without a clue what to do next. I was a hot mess.

Daily I began seeking God's counsel in the pages of my journal. Over and over I asked *Where do I go from here? What should I be doing? Isn't there a way I can use what I'm good at to be of value to the world without killing myself?*

Thankfully, God heard my heartfelt pleas, but before He revealed what I was next to do, He reminded me who and whose I am. He whispered in my ear that I was His beloved child, and His treasured possession. He showed me that before I was even born he created a plan for my life, and that it was good. He assured me of this one simple truth:

I am because He is, and because He is, anything is possible.

Those words gave me hope, and over time, they unlocked a series of powerful life lessons as God reconciled the disparate parts of myself back to Him. The lessons were so simple, and yet so profound in their application, because embracing them freed me from the rigid interpretation of how life *should* be and opened my eyes to a whole new world of what *could* be.

I stopped trying to stuff myself into the box of what I knew, based on my experience, credibility, and expertise. Instead, I ventured beyond my comfort zone and embraced God's great gift of life more abundantly. I learned to live by faith, to move forward in the direction He was leading despite my limitations, and to love the real me, the woman I was created to be—flaws, faults, and all.

At times it's been a wild and wacky adventure, and at other times it's been a lot of hard work. But it has all been worth it, as I have seen the impossible and unexplainable manifest in my life time and time again. Throughout my transformation, I've shared many of my experiences on the *Loving on Me* blog, and, to my delight, women from all walks of life have reached out in support. They've confided they too struggle with the very same thing as they search for the *more* they know life has in store.

That's why I'm so excited to share with you the lessons God poured into my spirit during my season of stillness. They're messages of love straight from my heart to yours, and I know beyond a shadow of a doubt that when you apply them, they will work wonders in your life too—not because I'm brilliant or an expert, but because I have experienced the power of them at work in my own life, and watched with awe and appreciation as God has done the same in the lives of others.

This book starts at the beginning of my ending, chronicling my journey from life-interrupted to living a life of abundance. I'll tell you up front—at times it is raw and unfiltered. I'm pretty candid about some of the crap I had to wade through and leave behind to get beyond my comfort zone.

But my goal isn't to impress you. My desire is for us to have an authentic conversation about what it takes to break free from the status quo. See, a lot of us have life-interrupted moments and miss the opportunity for a life change. We survive, but we don't take a moment to process, heal, or regroup so that we can thrive.

That's why I've included practical examples from my life, as well as comments other women have shared on the blog. I want you to understand how each experience presents us with an opportunity to consciously choose our path, and how it takes patience to let the process unfold. My hope is that, as you read our stories, you can hear God's voice whispering to you about your own, and be emboldened to courageously pursue a life beyond what you can hope or imagine.

Now, before we get started, let me tell you what you can expect. First, this is not a get-rich-quick scheme. Nor is it a blueprint for prosperity. Instead, consider this book your guide on a faith-filled journey to help you define you, based on who God created you to be, and to boldly move forward in fulfilling your divine assignment. Second, I am a woman of faith. This book is written from that foundation, and explores in large part how to put the faith that so many of us share into action.

So take your time and don't rush the experience. Read each chapter, and then grab a journal so you can write a bit, capturing observations about your own life. Trust me, I know you don't have all day, so the chapters aren't very long. But in order to get the most out of your experience, be sure to spend some time meditating on the affirmations throughout, opening your heart and head to a new way of thinking and a bolder way of living. You'll be amazed at what God deposits in your spirit when you're finally still enough to hear.

And when you feel intrigued but know what's in here is just not enough to get you started, check out the *Bookshelf Boosts* following each chapter. They feature links to some of my favorite books and resources, which, in the midst of my own confusion, offered great clarity and calm. I've learned quite a lot from people a little further down the path than I am. I suspect you will too.

It's going to be a grand adventure! Are you ready to get going? You bet you are! When you picked up this book, you took the first step. So come on … let's walk a spell together. ❧

LESSON ONE

I Am Enough

How can I be so smart and be in something so stupid?

Working as a senior executive at an international breast cancer charity, I was at the top of my professional game. Blessed with the rare opportunity to do what I loved while also making a difference, I was fiercely committed to the mission and incredibly proud of our life-changing work. Life wasn't perfect, but it was pretty darn sweet.

That is, until a fateful January day when what should have been a private discourse over funding erupted into a very public and heated debate with another women's nonprofit. It was an absolute spectacle fueled by nonstop media coverage and confusion. Within twenty-four hours, we went from being one of the world's most beloved charities to being engulfed by a raging wildfire, one we had absolutely no idea how to extinguish or control.

Every day, our offices around the country were besieged with thousands of angry calls and e-mails from donors who weren't happy with our decisions. Our national office was routinely under the threat of protest, and one day someone even took a shot at our building. Yep! You read it right: a gunshot. As you can imagine, when building security told us they were considering putting bulletproof film on the windows, "job security" took on a whole new meaning.

It was a catastrophe of the worst proportions—personally and professionally—especially for those of us trying to put out the flames. *Stressed* doesn't even begin to describe our state. For weeks on end, it was an all-day all-hands-on-deck fight. Regularly we'd spend twelve to fourteen hours each day at the office being attacked over the phone and e-mail, only to go home and find the same thing happening on our personal social media pages. It was exhausting and incredibly frustrating. Worse still was that while we worked hard to put out the fire, I personally began to suffocate from the smoke.

As news coverage of our crisis began including references to hidden agendas and covert agreements, my stress level went through the roof. And my internal angst started manifesting in some pretty severe outward symptoms. In the middle of meetings, my chest would suddenly tighten and my face would start tingling. My lips would go numb, and no matter how much I massaged, I couldn't make it go away. After a while, it started happening at night too, along with uncontrollable jerking as I slept.

Initially, I chalked it up to elevated blood pressure. Given the extreme circumstances, it seemed a reasonable conclusion. I assumed things would go back to normal when the crisis had passed. But there were moments—actually a lot of moments—when I wondered if I were having a heart attack and a stroke at the same time.

After weeks of nonstop mania, I finally gave in to my son's pleas and went to see the doctor. I had almost blacked out while exercising, and the incident scared him half to death. Isn't it ridiculous that I, who had been working in healthcare marketing for over fifteen years and had created campaigns around taking charge of your health, had to be harassed by my child to stop what I was doing and take care of me?

The irony would hit me many months later, not to mention the foolishness of running around thinking I might be having a heart attack and not going to see a doctor! Clearly, my life priorities had gotten completely out of whack.

The great news is that when the doctor came in with the test results, he confirmed I wasn't having a heart attack or a stroke. Instead, he told me I was having anxiety attacks and hyperventilating, nearly all day, every day. I stared at him in disbelief, trying to absorb the news. Surely, he must be wrong. I didn't have problems with anxiety. I was a single parent, had been through a messy divorce, and faced any number of challenges in my life—all without being brought to my knees. There's no way this had gotten the better of me. He must have missed something in the tests.

But when I began to question him, he explained it more clearly. "You're right," he said. "I've been your doctor for twenty years, and I know you don't normally have anxiety issues. What you have now is an environmental issue, and at this point, it's time for you to make a change."

He tried to take me off work for a month, but I wouldn't hear of it. I couldn't leave in the middle of a crisis. They needed me. "Well, how about two weeks?" he asked. "Just long enough for you to get some rest and think things through."

I tried to wrap my brain around walking in and telling the team at work that I needed a medical leave, but I just couldn't do it. How would they maintain any hope if leadership bowed out of the fight?

As I drove back to the office, I felt very dejected. I kept asking myself over and over, *How did I let myself get here, in a place I don't recognize and—worse yet—can't control?* Huh. Maybe that was the problem. In trying to control everything, I eventually controlled nothing—not even me.

We busy women tend to do that, you know. We feel compelled to run everything and to fix everybody. But so often, it is the care and feeding of ourselves that we leave sorely lacking, which is why, even after the doctor told me to take a break, I dove right back in, determined to patch things up before I got some rest.

However, as the days unfolded, my anxiety continued to increase. The more I tried to fix things, the more frustrated I became that circumstances remained the same. So I prayed about it, sought some advice from my mentors, and eventually made the tough decision that my time there had come to an end. I stepped aside and resigned.

It was one of the toughest choices of my life, but in doing so, I learned a valuable lesson.

> *I can choose my path, even when I can't change the circumstances.*

Boy, was that a bitter pill to swallow, because the fixer in me desperately wanted to stick around to see us get back on the right path. Surely I was smart enough to help figure it out. That was my thing.

By "thing" I mean that quality that defines us and sets us apart among our peers. It's what people know they can expect from us and what makes us feel good about ourselves. It starts when we're kids and continues throughout our adult lives. Some are told they're pretty, creative, or great in sports. Others are compassionate or strong. Me? I have always been smart, and in business that translated to being a strategic thinker who could figure stuff out and get things done.

I don't share this with you to brag, but merely as an explanation to why my self-esteem was rooted in being smart. You see, most of us spend our whole lives trying to live up to or live down the labels placed on us as children. Rarely is it that we are instilled with value purely as human beings, but rather for what we can do or accomplish in this lifetime, as compared to other people. As a result, we often let one element of our makeup define our whole self-worth.

I know that's pretty much what I did. So imagine my disappointment at being the "smart" girl embroiled in such a stupid mess. As one of the senior executives, I should have been able to stop this, shouldn't I? *What will people say about me, and will they respect me once they find out I've resigned? They'll probably think I just up and quit because it got difficult. I'll never get another job. My stock price will be zero dollars.*

It seems so dramatic as I write it. But when I listen to other women's stories, I hear much the same tale.

> *I was laid off after working in HR for twenty years. How could they, when I've given them everything? I so want to do something different, but I'm over fifty and afraid it's too late to pursue something new. No one wants to hire someone old like me.*

> *We were married for ten years before things fell apart. I should have seen this coming! Now I'm past my prime and gained a little weight. I'm not as cute as I used to be. No one will want me for a wife again.*

It all sounds so over the top, but truthfully, this is often our first response to change. When we can't go on doing what we used to do, or—heaven forbid—we have to pull off our Superwoman mask and just be who we are, what's in front of us can seem like insurmountable odds. We panic and many times discount our ability to do anything, because we allow our past or present circumstances to make us feel like we have nothing. Sometimes, we feel that we ourselves are nothing, with very little value to offer the world.

It can be a vulnerable, scary place that paralyzes us with fear of the unknown. But it can also be a season of incredible breakthrough. It really comes down to the standard we choose for determining our value and worth.

Honestly, I struggled with this. The public censure and private shame created a heavy load, and most days I felt like I was carrying it alone. Too embarrassed to talk about my health issues and not sure how to explain what happened to cause the eruption at work, I ended up isolating myself from most of my friends and family. I felt like a failure, largely due to my inability to control people and circumstances that were out of my control.

Isn't it amazing how often our hearts can be in the right places, but our hands are at work in spaces where God never intended? I suspect it's because we secretly believe we can control everything. But then a life-interrupted moment happens, reminding us that we can't. So to keep our illusion of control in place, we chastise ourselves for not doing more, rather than facing the reality that some circumstances are out of control.

However, the truth is there are some things in life we are not meant to change, fix, or handle. I know that's an unpopular notion in today's take charge culture, but of this I'm sure—taking on mantles of responsibility that are not our own locks us in an endless cycle of feeling less than, frustrated and unworthy. We cannot control every circumstance, and certainly not other people—nor are we meant to, which is why we have to learn to identify and address our own mess, while allowing others to do the same.

It can be tough to know when we're out of balance in this area when our swirling emotions have left us feeling empty and confused. But blessedly, God sends us who and what we need right when we need it, someone or something that holds a mirror before us, pointing out what our minds won't let our eyes see.

For me, that was a doctor friend from Africa. We hadn't known each other for very long, but he's one of those folks you recognize from the start as a kindred spirit. After days of watching my mounting worry, anxiety, and self-judgment from afar, he sent me this e-mail:

> *I want you to write this on a note and post it somewhere you can see it every day. Read it, say it out loud, and believe it—because it most assuredly is true.*

> **I am enough.**

To be honest, I wasn't feeling it at first. I was sick, tired, and frustrated. There was nothing about me that felt "enough." All I could see was what I wasn't.

But he kept at me until I agreed to try it. Eventually, every time I felt worried, upset or out of control, I would quietly whisper to myself over and over "I Am Enough." But then another voice in my head kept saying, why? Why are you enough?

Hmm ... why am I enough? I had to ponder on that, because if I looked at the destruction from the wildfire, there didn't seem to be a lot left. So much of what I had poured my heart and soul into building over the last six years lay smoldering at my feet. Clearly, what I had done had not been enough.

But one morning when I was talking to God in the pages of my journal, the Spirit deposited a word of comfort: *You are His beloved child, and that's why you are enough.* Yes! That was it. I *am* enough. Not because of what I do or how much I accomplish in this life. Not because I get it right all the time, or am oh so smart. And certainly not because I have super powers to control everything and everybody. Simply because I am God's beloved child, I am enough.

Oh, how I wish I could convey to you the relief and joy that floods my soul every time I think about being God's child. Even now tears come to my eyes when I reflect on how grateful and blessed I felt in that moment, because that reminder that my value and worth come from Him relieved me from the constant pressure of trying to earn it.

See, here's the thing—we're going to mess up, and every now and again feel lost and confused. Life is full of ups and downs. Some days we'll be soaring, and other times we'll crash and burn. Hard. But if our standard for self-worth is in who we are, not what we do, we can stay balanced even in turbulent times.

This is why it's so important that we truly understand who God says we are: a masterpiece made in His image, His treasured possession, and the apple of His eye. We are divinely purposed, more than conquerors, and destined to do great things. He loves us so much that we are never alone, and we can always depend on Him.

In the midst of the fire, those words became my oxygen. Over and over I meditated on what He said about me. Each time it was like taking a breath of fresh air—renewing my resolve to appreciate me as I am, and to know that what God made me is enough.

As I look back on it, I realize that what I was doing was reprogramming my thinking. I'm sure there is a scientific name for it, but I like to think of it as breaking the cycle of negativity by replacing the narrative. ***Speaking kindly to me, based on what***

God said, not what I saw, gave me hope. It helped me reaffirm my worth as a human being, in spite of the present circumstances.

I offer that same assurance to you. It doesn't matter if your life-interrupted moment is a normal course of life or an unplanned catastrophe. It doesn't matter if you're lost and confused, or know your next step. You are enough—without a job, without a title, or what you perceive to be an "important" task. You are a beloved Child of God, and that is what gives our lives meaning. The things we assumed made us of value are but mere manifestations of our being.

We struggle with this concept because we're so desperate to be better or best at something. However, if we embrace the notion that all human life is endowed with value from the moment it is created, it would cause a cataclysmic shift in our thinking. If we truly believed that we all came here as enough, it would set us free.

You see, when I understood that I am enough, I gradually stopped comparing my life to anyone else's, or to who I used to be. I started letting go of the pre-prescribed notion of how life was supposed to unfold, and I just lived it. I allowed for the impossible and unexplainable to take shape as life evolved according to the divine plan.

But those changes didn't happen overnight. I had to constantly feed myself positive messages to replace the negative loop running through my mind. That's how I fell in love with affirmations. They were short, sweet messages from me to me, little reminders to keep my thoughts on track and my eyes focused on the future rather than the past.

Most were just a sentence or two, but eventually I put a few together to write my own life affirmation so that even now, when the ups and downs come, as they most assuredly will, I won't be overwhelmed. I'll have an anchor that defines who I am, even when I'm not sure what to do.

I encourage you to write your own too. Post it somewhere prominent so you can see it everyday. That way you never lose sight of you. I've posted mine below to help you get started. ❧

I am a beloved child of God.
I am here for a unique purpose, something only I can do.
I am gifted beyond what I can imagine.
I am more valuable than I can measure.
I am strong, I am mighty, I am enough.

BOOKSHELF *boost*

Still wondering how you can be sure you are enough? Let our Creator set the standard. Find out what God says about you in my free eBook *21 Affirmations for Loving the Real You*. It's a twenty-one-day meditation that lays out what God thinks about you— and why you can be assured that you are indeed enough.

Visit http://lovingonme.com/21-affirmations/ to download your free copy. You can also sign up for our free newsletter, delivering a weekly dose of positive inspiration to your inbox.

LESSON TWO

I Am Worthy

How will they get this done without me?

Oliver Wendell Holmes, Sr., said, "One's mind, once stretched by a new idea, never regains its original dimensions." I think that is especially true when our life is enlightened by God's truths, because the more we understand them, the more our attitudes and actions in every aspect of our lives change.

We begin to examine the intentions behind our actions as we seek to bring all of our life in line with our Creator. It's a journey in search of something more, but in order to reach it, we have to leave some things behind and release them for good. And as I soon discovered, this is where the real work begins.

I resigned in February, but didn't actually leave my job until May. My "generosity" in giving a three-month notice went against the counsel of my mentors, but it's what felt fair and right to me. I told myself I didn't want to leave the organization in a lurch, that I needed to deliver a plan for recovery before I departed. And while that was how I genuinely felt, it definitely wasn't the whole story.

Truth is, I really did want to help set the course even if I wasn't going to be there to help lead us through to the other side. However, why I thought I had to be the one to do so was a combination of guilt, ego, and a misplaced sense of responsibility to rescue. Yep! I'm a rescuer, and once again I was making myself the victim and hero all wrapped up in one.

It's taken me many years to see this pattern in my life, and honestly, had it not been for my transition coach, I probably still wouldn't acknowledge it as true. But over time she was able to help me see the role that I had given myself—peacemaker, cleanup master, go between, and savior—were not functions I needed to own. In fact, this compulsive need to control and fix things was what was making me sick in the first place.

Sadly, this wasn't the first time in my life I had taken on this role. When my coach compared my relationship with my work colleagues to the one I had with my ex-husband, it was like a punch to the gut, because once my unhealthy, co-dependent marriage came to an end I vowed never to make those mistakes again. And yet here I was, trying to control and fix things that weren't my responsibility.

I know some of you are reading this thinking, *That has nothing to do with me. I don't rescue people. I've never been in an unhealthy relationship or felt like I needed to control everything.* Well, that may be true, but just in case you're wondering, see if any of these scenarios strike a chord with you …

> *A loved one drinks too much. They always call you to help them out of their little foibles. You're sick of*

*the situation, but **you're the only one who cares**, so you keep doing it.*

*An adult child is constantly in a financial bind. It's not their fault. They can't find a good job, and when they do their boss always treats them unfairly. You want them off your dime, but you keep giving them a little extra, because **if you don't help**, who will?*

*At the office, they always ask at the last minute when they need your help. You're frustrated and angry because it throws your schedule in a lurch, but you don't say anything. **There's no one else** who can do it like you can. So you suck it up, again.*

*Your spouse depends on you for everything, even the simple stuff they should be able to do on their own. You're constantly irritated and annoyed, but you **don't feel like there's anything you can do** to change the situation. That's just the way they are, and they need you to hold everything together.*

Those thoughts sound familiar? Most people I meet have at some time or another had at least one co-dependent relationship. We slip into them so easily for three reasons:

- We believe we're the only one who can do it, or that we do it best.
- We're convinced no one else cares, including the person we're trying to rescue.
- We feel good about it. Rescuing makes us feel important, needed—and here's the big one—loved!

Those are the things that go through our minds as we're doing things that deep down we don't want to do, but emotionally feel like we have to do. Our self-esteem and self-worth become wrapped up in the doing, and as a result, we go to the absolute extreme to satisfy our need to be needed.

That pretty much sums up my story. Day after day, as we worked to develop the recovery plan, I became more and more discontent. It had nothing to do with the people around me. It was just time for me to let go, and everybody knew it.

You see, there were two fatal flaws in my thinking. First, no matter how I "felt," God had already told me it was time for me to go. Staying put me out of sync with His will, and there can never be contentment when you're not in line with Him.

We often try to put God's plans on our timing, especially when it comes to big changes in our lives. But there is a heavy price to be paid for doing so, especially in our peace of mind. I believe **God is most pleased with us when we are obedient, immediately.** Oh, how much easier life would be if we accepted that His timing is perfect, even when we don't see the plan.

However, our fears of the future often overwhelm us. We want to know what's next before we let go of what we have. So we stay where we feel respected, valued, or needed rather than responding to the call to take a grand leap of faith. But here's a little secret, and it's the root of the second flaw I uncovered in my thinking:

> *Just because you feel needed doesn't mean they really need you.*

Ouch! That one stung just writing it. But it's true. When God allows an ending in our life, it creates a ripple effect in the lives of those around us. Not only are we in transition, but things are changing for them too. It's as if the entire universe as we know it is experiencing a seismic shift, and the space we used to inhabit no longer exists.

That's why the role we used to play just a few days before now doesn't fit. We keep trying to insert ourselves back in the game, but in many ways we've become irrelevant, causing an unnecessary tension in the environment. It's ironic, but eventually the very people we're trying to help—meaning rescue—come to resent us. Why? Because our "loving" presence is stifling their growth!

But when we accept as fact that we are valuable, purely because we are beloved children of God, created in His image and designed for a purpose, then we don't have to try and hold on to what was. We can let go so that everyone can grow, moving forward with confidence into our new normal.

Has God told you it's time to go? Perhaps for you it's not a physical departure like mine. It could be that He's urging you to release an old way of thinking. Either way, if you sense Him calling you to a season of stillness, change, or redirection I encourage you to **choose to follow His plan and say YES!**

Sometimes we don't get all the answers of what's next up front, but we can believe and trust in God's plans. Just like He had one for me, He had one for all the people I didn't want to leave behind. At the time, I just didn't trust Him enough to be obedient immediately, and I didn't love myself enough to do what was best for me.

Ultimately, by staying longer, I think I was trying to earn my own love and respect. Yes, I cared about other people, deeply. But I also needed to be needed in order to feel useful.

Now I work hard to keep a healthy balance between my compassionate spirit and my desire to take over and control things. I understand my pattern of falling into co-dependent relationships, and I am careful to seek God's direction before I intervene. The funny thing is, when I resist the urge to take over, I've found people figure things out on their own just fine.

These days, when I feel myself trying to hold on when God is telling me to let go, I remind myself I don't have to earn His love or my own. I don't have to create value for my life by trying to fix things or do things He has not called me to do. I am enough just as I am, and I can love me for me. So can you.

Write this in the front of your journal or notepad so that you see it each day:

I am worthy of my own love and respect.
I don't have to earn it by doing things I am not called to do.
I just have to believe it, and receive it.
God loves me, and so can I.

Now I want you to take a moment for self-reflection. Are there areas where you need to let go? What's holding you back? Are your hands at work where you have no business? The only way we can be better is if we learn to be honest with our selves about what's really happening in our lives.

Sometimes we blame stagnation on our circumstances, when in truth it's really our lack of self-assessment that is the issue. So today I want you to use your journal to look in the mirror and talk to you. Like I did above, ask yourself why you are doing the things you're doing. Be honest about whether you want to do them, or feel like you have to do them. Do you feel they're fulfilling a purpose, or are they filling your need to be needed?

Let's be honest about where we are and establish a baseline for our growth. Now, don't spend any time judging you. This is not about beating yourself up. And for now, don't worry about how to stop doing what you're doing. That will come in due season. In fact, for some of you, just writing it out and seeing on paper how and where you've been spending your time is going to be such an eye-opener no further discussion will be required. Truth has a way of snapping us out of merely going through the motions.

But if that's not you, don't worry about it. It took me a while to get this too, and even now I still feel my propensity to rescue rear its ugly little head. That control issue takes some work as well. The beautiful thing is, these life lessons keep me grounded and provide a constant reminder that I am enough, and I am worthy. If you allow them, they'll do the same thing for you.

So meditate on the affirmation you wrote in the front of your journal, stay encouraged, and keep going! The journey gets sweeter and sweeter by and by. ❥

If you struggle with rescuing, I've got a resource for you. Pick up Melody Beattie's *Co-Dependent No More: How to Stop Controlling Others and Start Caring for You*. It was life changing for me, and for everyone I recommended it to.

Grab a copy at http://katrinamcghee.com/books/.

LESSON THREE

I Am Purposed

God, what do you want me to do with me?

Life-interrupted moments can be tough because they often trigger an ending without providing a clear pathway for a new beginning. Even when we're grounded in who we are and who is charting our course, we can still wander for a while, making it hard to patiently wait for our next steps. This is why God sometimes sends us a bit of encouragement in the midst of our chaos and confusion.

He restores our peace by unexpectedly giving us a peek at what's to come. It usually occurs when our minds are at rest, and we're finally still enough to pay attention. Such an experience happened for me one night as I was sleeping.

I remember having a dream so vivid that it felt like it was happening in real time. There was a huge fire. It was so intense

I could feel the heat from the flames. As the fire died down, out of it emerged a giant flying creature with beautiful brilliant red and gold coloring across its entire body and wings. Just as it was taking flight, I awoke, and I knew at once that I had witnessed a phoenix rising from the ashes.

The interesting thing is I had no idea how I knew. The words meant nothing to me, and yet the concept seemed oddly familiar. I looked it up online and discovered the phoenix rising is actually a pretty famous story from Greek mythology. As its been told through the centuries, the phoenix is destined to go through a cyclical rebirth. It begins with a great fire, which consumes the entire bird, except for its very essence, which is safely encased within an egg.

Nestled inside the fire's ashes, the egg is kept warm until the phoenix is ready to be reborn. When it emerges, the new bird has the best of what was and everything it needs for the next phase of life. It is a glorious sight as it takes flight—whole, purposed, and complete.

Wow! That sounded so much like what we were going through. What an encouragement! Surely God had sent this message as a sign that if we stayed focused on our core, everything was going to be okay. We would not only survive, we'd rise again—better, stronger, and repurposed for the road ahead.

By "we" I meant the organization. It was months before I recognized it was a personal message for me too. Just like the phoenix, I could see how God had used the same wildfire that rocked my world to get rid of aspects of my life that had no place in my future. But that was a hindsight view—as in after I survived, turned a corner, and could look back without getting angry all over again.

When I was fighting the flames ... that hurt like hell! I bet some of you know what I'm talking about. In an instant, the well-made plans we've spent years building can all but disappear, and we can't do a thing about it.

> *The company you've been with for twenty years suddenly announces they've outsourced your entire department. You were planning to retire in another five years.*

> *Your boyfriend of three years walks in and tells you he's marrying someone else. You had your whole life planned together, and now you're alone.*

> *You got hurt on the job, and now you can't work. The career you love is over. It's so unfair that what you're really good at has been taken away.*

Life sure can suck, can't it? I mean, intellectually we know when bad things happen it's not the end of our story. After all, we're still here. But emotionally, we're a wreck, having been hurt to the core. So how can we confidently move on when: a) we don't know where we're supposed to go, and b) what we thought was the foundation we'd use to springboard to our next phase of life crumbles?

Well, I think first we have to remind ourselves everything in life lasts only for a season, and seasons are meant to change. Those circumstances we want to remain as they are were in fact produced by a previous change in our life. So we can be assured the one we're experiencing now, as painful as it may be, is really just the bridge taking us to the next phase of our journey.

Second, we can be encouraged knowing that God is not the author of chaos and confusion. Everything He created has purpose, meaning, and order. And nature itself—the birds, plants and animals—are all a constant reminder of His plan for how change triggers rebirth and renewal.

God has a way of taking our bitter or unexpected endings and turning them into our best beginnings. The disappointing things that happen in our lives are only a part of our story, and no matter how bad they are, we can rise again—different, better, and much, much stronger. We just have to be patient and trust Him, knowing we're moving on to higher ground.

About a month after dreaming about the phoenix, I finally took a week off. Wish I could say it was because good sense finally kicked in, but truth is, I was exhausted. Even though I'd resigned, I was still working like I had plans to stay forever.

See, that was my pattern—go until I couldn't go any more. A lot of you do it too. We run on fumes until our tank is cleaned out, knowing full well we should have stopped eons ago to refuel. But of course there's always something more important than ourselves. That is, until our bodies revolt and force us to reconsider our priorities.

Which is exactly what I did. As I sat on the swing in my backyard, I began to think about my future. No one believed I was leaving my job without a plan, but I knew the road ahead stretched endlessly before me like the Sahara Desert. No signs pointed the way, and there was nothing I was particularly passionate about.

I needed some time alone with God so I could find my way. One thing is for sure, I could not have made it without Him. Throughout my transition, which publicly lasted for months and privately for years, it was my relationship with God that kept me safe and sane. On days when I was at my lowest, it was Psalm 23 which played continuously through my mind.

The Lord is my shepherd,
I shall not want.
He makes me lie down in green pastures;
He leads me beside quiet waters.
He restores my soul;
He guides me in the paths of righteousness
For His name's sake.
Even though I walk through the valley of the shadow
of death,
I fear no evil, for You are with me.
Your rod and Your staff, they comfort me.
You prepare a table before me in the presence of my
enemies;
You have anointed my head with oil;
My cup overflows.
Surely goodness and loving kindness will follow me
all the days of my life,
And I will dwell in the house of the Lord forever.[1]

For me, those were so much more than just verses in the Bible. I was living them, in excruciating detail. My faith—which I had taken for granted for years—was being tested in a whole new way, and God's love and care meant more to me than ever before.

You see, I'd been a Christian since I was a kid. I loved God, went to church, paid tithes, prayed, and dedicated my life to helping others. And yet, I wasn't what anyone would call overtly religious. Many people weren't even familiar with this part of my life. But still, I pretty much checked all the boxes.

Before my life-interrupted moment got my attention, my kinship with God had become more of a religious experience

---

[1] Psalm 23 NASB

based on following the rules instead of a relationship built on love. I had been missing out on the best part, and I didn't even know it.

But those alone moments on the swing helped me create an intimate space with Him. It helped me understand why Christ so often went off alone to pray. It's not that we have to be by ourselves to talk to God, but when we are, it allows us to focus our whole selves on communing with Him.

Writing in my journal helped me do that too. It gave me a way to pour out my heart to Him and diligently seek His response. It also helped me sift through my vacillating thoughts and emotions and suss out what was most important, for this season. The interesting thing is, no one thing came to mind. I had no idea what to ask for, so instead **I chose to ask for what He wanted for me**.

*God I want to do what **you** want me to do. I don't care if it's another job, a business, serving as a missionary, or something weird I've never heard of. Just point me in the right direction and I'll go. I just ask for one thing: an extraordinary life that only you can do.*

I could hear His voice, like a whisper to my heart, responding almost immediately.

- It's going to be more than you can imagine.
- It will touch millions of lives.
- It'll transform the world.

Now, let me stop for a moment and be real honest. Up until this season in my life, I had no idea what God's voice sounded like, and even now I can't imitate it or describe it in detail. Yes, He had communicated with me through dreams. He'd sent me messages through sermons, through other people, and by reading His word. But hear His voice? Never. And yet, when He spoke, I knew it was God. I recognized it just like a child knows the voice of its parents, or a creation that is forever linked to its Creator.

As quirky as it sounds—and believe me, I know some of you are reading this with a really healthy dose of skepticism—I don't think this is a strange phenomenon. In fact, I think God speaks to us all the time. If I were to guess why most of us believe we've never had the experience of hearing Him, I'd say it's probably for one of two reasons: a) we're too busy to stop and listen, or b) when we do hear Him, we don't believe what He's telling us.

You know why? Because when God starts talking, stuff can get a little scary. The picture he paints of our lives is always so much *bigger* than we could dream up on our own, so we feel a little lost and unsure of ourselves, not knowing whether to believe it or what to do next.

That's why sometimes we'll convince ourselves we didn't hear what we heard, and then try to squeeze back into situations we know are too small for our spirit. It allows us to maintain our illusion of bigness without ever going through the tough stuff so we can grow.

Like when we feel strongly that God is directing us to be an entrepreneur, but we're frightened we won't be able to make it financially, so we stick with our full-time job; or when he tells us to let go of a relationship, but we're afraid to be alone; or when he tells us to forgive someone, but we decide they don't deserve it. We think we're making the logical and safe choice, but really we're just running scared.

I had done that before, but this time I made up my mind I wasn't having it! I wanted more. So instead of taking my plans to God, I wanted Him to reveal His plans for me. It was time for me to put my faith in action. I realized that if I ever wanted to truly be all that I was created to be and have a lasting peace within myself,

I had best get on the same page as my Creator. I chose to follow God, even if it meant getting out of my comfort zone.

Man, I wish I hadn't had to get so sick to see things clearly. But then again, when would I have stopped to even consider if I were on the right path, especially since my work was so rewarding? Did I really have to fear for my life before I heard God's voice?

I don't think so. Truthfully, I think God had been signaling that it was time for a change for quite a while. I just hadn't stopped long enough to pay attention to his subtle cues. But going back through some of my older journals, I realized that my panic attacks had happened before. They were mild and I had no idea what they were, but they were annoying enough that I made note of them. And to no surprise, those were also brought on by job-related events.

At the time I remember thinking, *It's time for me to leave.* But I couldn't figure out where to go. Nothing else seemed as grand as what I was already doing. So rather than taking some time to pray about it and seek God's direction, I pushed those feelings to the side and stayed, only to have the very same warning signs resurface again in a way that couldn't be ignored.

I know some of you just read that and immediately thought about how God has been trying to get your attention. You've had warning signs galore, and, like me, you've been ignoring them because you can't see what more God has in store. I was stuck there for a long time too. But you know what I discovered was the key to moving forward? Surrender.

Surrender of my will to His. Surrender of what I thought I had to have to what God knew I needed. Surrender of who I worked so hard to become to who He was calling me to be.

Believe me, I know it's not easy to relinquish control. After all, we work hard for the life we want, and the thought of giving it up can be overwhelming, especially when we don't know that what we'll get in return will be better. I'm certain that's why, up until this point, I had held on to parts of my life that seemed to be on track. I mean, why would I ask God what He wants done with my career when it's going just fine?

But, you see, that's our critical mistake. We beg God for help when we're broke down. We come to Him crying our eyes out when stuff falls apart. But when life is good, we want to be left alone. We're not interested in His plans, because our plans are on track. Trouble is, when our plans go awry, we can't always fix them. And then we don't know what to do but run back to God and beg Him to bless our mess.

But this time I'm challenging you to do things a little differently. You're at a crossroads, wanting more for your life but not sure what that *more* is. It's a season pregnant with possibility, presenting the perfect opportunity to step out on faith. So instead of racing around in every direction trying to come up with a plan, why not courageously join me in asking God what plans He has for you? Let Him lead the way. After all, He's already told you He has a plan for your life:

> *For I know the plans I have for you, declares the Lord, plans to prosper you and not to harm you, plans to give you hope and a future.*[2]

And he's already told you how to access it:

> *Trust in the Lord with all your heart, and lean not on your own understanding; In all your ways acknowledge Him, and He shall direct your paths.*[3]

---

[2] Jeremiah 29:11 NIV
[3] Proverbs 3:5–6 NKJV

So what's the problem? Oh wait—I know. It's that relationship thing, right? We know about God, but we don't really know God, and because we don't, we can't begin to trust Him with our lives. Which is a real shame, since at the end of the day He's the only one who knows it all.

Well, here's the good news—God wants a relationship with you too. He wants you to really get to know Him. If you're a Christian, he's waiting for you to spend more time with Him. Get in the habit of seeking Him out each day. You can buy a devotional to guide you or download one of the numerous apps available to lead you through getting to know God better.

If you're not a Christian, or don't know if you are, then I invite you into the family. If you want a life of abundance—full, rich, and rewarding—it starts with accepting the free gift of salvation. See, God loves us so much that, more than anything, He wants a relationship with us. But the thing is, he's holy, and, well, we're not. Even the best of us are a sinful lot.

So in order for us to have a direct connection with Him, it required a sacrifice, and that was his son, Jesus. He died for us so we could be set free from all the crap we've been carrying around. All we have to do is believe it, accept His gift of salvation, and ask Him to live in our hearts.

But wait—what about our guilt, shame, and sinful ways? The awesome news is when we accept Him, He forgives it all. From that moment on, we're saved.

Sound simple? Good, because it really is. Listen, I have to be honest, I didn't start out to write a book about salvation. And I know I've probably lost some of you. I've suddenly gotten too religious, and you didn't buy this book to be preached at.

Trust me, if it were up to me, much to my chagrin, I would probably skip this part too. Truth be told, this is the first time in my Christian life I have *ever* been compelled to try to explain salvation in this public a fashion. But my spirit would not let me rest without talking about it, so I guess this is a growth point for me too.

Here's the thing, I couldn't figure out how you could possibly take the next step on this journey without a personal relationship with God. He's our anchor when life's storms are raging and our guide when the way seems dark. He's who we go to when we don't know where to go, and I find that when we go to Him with an open head and heart, He reveals things to us in a way that calms our fears and makes us excited about the road ahead.

Go ahead and trust Him. Believe in Him and surrender. Surrender by letting go of what you think you want and asking Him for what He knows you need. Quit pushing your agenda, and be open to His plan. And then be ready to follow it—even to the ends of the earth.

Take a moment and meditate on the phrase below. Allow it to encourage you in the days ahead, when you're tempted to ignore the signs, run scared, or settle back in where you've already been. Spend some time developing your relationship with Him and begin talking to Him in the pages of your journal.

Perhaps a good way to start is by writing out your prayers. Why don't you make the first one about patience? If you've made the decision to surrender, more than likely this will be an area of struggle. In fact, it's where many of us stray from the path, because it can take a while for our desires to get in line with our destiny. But we can be victorious if we learn not to rush and instead be ready.

When you're tempted to run ahead, remember the phoenix rising. Stay safely nestled within the ashes until God calls you to break free. Before you know it, you'll be flying again—stronger and better than you were before. ♥

I am purposed and God has a plan.
I am who He says I am.
I will trust in Him!

BOOKSHELF *boost*

If you want to know more about developing a relationship with God and what salvation really means, here are some scriptures to get you started on your journey: John 3:16, Romans 3:23, Romans 6:23, Romans 5:8, and Romans 10:9-10. If you don't have a Bible at home, use the Internet to research and read them in multiple translations.

Listen, don't get discouraged if you don't understand everything right away. Getting to know God takes a lifetime, and the more time you spend with Him, the more He reveals himself to you. To help understand what you're reading, I recommend going to a local Christian bookstore and asking for suggestions on a good study Bible. That will give you context for what you're reading and clarity on how to apply it.

LESSON FOUR

I Am Guided

Why did I stand up when I know God told me to sit down?

When we know we're on a path to someplace new, but we're not really sure where we're going, we get a lot of well-meaning advice to try to steer us back from where we came. It's inevitable, because people tend to be uncomfortable with the undefined. It's not that they're opposed to us growing. They just need us to get somewhere in a hurry so they can compartmentalize us in a way that makes sense in relation to their own lives.

Well, that doesn't really work when living a life of surrender. Sadly, God doesn't wave a magic wand and suddenly change our life. Nope, instead he transforms us from the inside out. And how long our transition takes often depends on how well we listen—which for me was a wee bit of a struggle.

By the time I reached my last day of work, I felt like I had been working on this transformation thing forever! But truthfully, I was just getting started. The next eighteen months would prove to be some of the hardest of my life. Coming and going, I had to reconcile me with myself as I learned to love and accept the real me.

However, before I got too far down the road, I decided to mark the moment with a little fun. I went on a skydiving adventure with my son and my dad. I know you're wondering, so I'll go ahead and say it—yes, we're all a little nuts. As my brother and sister-in-law told us, there was no reason to jump out of a perfectly good airplane. Yet, somehow, I reasoned in my mind, this was an appropriate way to punctuate the close of this season and celebrate my grand leap of faith into the next. Turns out, it was also an incredible foreshadowing of what was to come.

Now, if you've never succumbed to a moment of madness and tried skydiving, let me tell you a bit about my experience. I and the other lunatics (excuse me, skydivers) were taken up in a small propeller airplane with no seats to about thirteen thousand feet. When we were above the landing site, the side door of the airplane was flung open and I, along with the expert who was strapped to me, was the first to jump out of the plane.

I use the term "jump" purely as a figure of speech. Because I'm telling you, when I swung my legs out of the open door and dared to look down, a form of terror previously unknown to me flooded my entire body. Whether I actually jumped willingly or had help exiting the plane, I'll never know, but in a matter of seconds we began tumbling at breakneck speed as our bodies hurtled toward the earth.

It felt like we were completely out of control, but fortunately my tandem partner knew how to manage our descent. He quickly stopped our head-over-heels motion and placed our bodies in a face-down horizontal position, allowing me to see all around, even though I couldn't hear a word—that is, until the parachute opened.

When the cord was pulled to release the chute, we jerked back up in the air another thousand feet or so. Shockingly, in the very same place where we previously couldn't hear a word, there was now utter stillness. It's a quiet like I've never experienced before, with the sounds around us being solely those we made. Can you imagine being in a space where the only signs of life are your own?

I could have floated up there for hours. But suddenly I looked down, and the ground was a lot closer than I had thought. I had to raise my legs to get ready to run as soon as I found my footing. Then, just like that, it was over, and we left to get on with the rest of our day. The funny thing is, had I not purchased a video, I couldn't have described the whole experience, because to this day, I can't actually remember the first thirty seconds of the fall.

Leaving the job I loved after six years of giving it my all was a lot like jumping out of the airplane. The shock of something that had been such a significant part of my life suddenly coming to an end overwhelmed my system and put me in what felt like an emotional free fall. For weeks I felt numb and out of sorts as I tried to find my footing.

To my surprise, I was grieving, and at times it engulfed me. Up until this experience, I had never really considered the fact that any ending, not just death, could result in grief. But that is surely what I felt. It wasn't because I wished I had stayed, but because my life as I knew it had died. It was gone in the blink of an eye, and the worst part was, the world was going on as if nothing happened. Even my friends—who loved me dearly—expected me to do the same.

That became painfully clear when a couple weeks later I left for an extended stay in Ghana. My trip was for two reasons. First and foremost, I needed a change of environment. I wanted to rest and think about my next move. And second, I had been invited to attend a breast cancer walk that I had helped start the year before.

When I first arrived, it felt like I had come back home. But after a few days I realized things had changed. They were still the same loving, caring community of friends that had become my second family, but I was different. I didn't quite fit in, not in the same way. Without my title and the backing of an organization to give me credibility, I felt awkward and out of place. I was an interloper in my own skin.

It reminds me of how I've heard so many other women describe their own life events. Being suddenly single again after years of marriage. Or feeling outside the action in retirement, or out of the club when you get laid off or your children leave home for college. When the designation we use to describe ourselves changes, it forces us to reexamine who we are without it, and by default, it forces those around us to do the same.

The interesting thing is they don't want to. Our well-meaning friends and family want us to be the same person we were to them before, but we can't, because our support system is gone. We're busy trying to learn how to function in our new normal, and they're often ready for us to go on with life.

That's why it wasn't really all that surprising when my friends asked me to speak at the upcoming walk. It's what I would normally have done in my previous role as an international delegate. And despite not working with the organization, they still wanted me to operate in that capacity.

I'm sure I shocked them when I immediately said no. Not only did I no longer want to occupy that space, I was certain God was calling me out of it into a place of stillness and silence. Although speaking was one of my God-given gifts, it was time to be quiet.

I needed to heal, regroup, and, honestly, find my own voice before I could begin speaking again.

The challenge was that this new me was so different than the person I had been. No one was ready to accept it. They argued that I could speak as just me. I didn't need an organization to define me. I would be respected without it. But I knew that wasn't true, because, honestly, I didn't respect me without it.

We went round and round, until two days before the event, I finally acquiesced and agreed to say a few words. I just couldn't let them down by coming all that way and not say something. Yep! My propensity to rescue rather than be real about how I was feeling kicked in again.

The night before the race, I wracked my brain trying to figure out what to say. As morning dawned, I was filled with a sense of dread. I should have pulled out. I really should have, because never in my life had God not deposited words into my spirit before I spoke. But I didn't want to let people down, so I stuck with the plan.

Well, that three-minute speech turned out to be the worst of my life. With thirty thousand people in the stands, I bombed. I struggled to get a few words out, but it turned out to be one of those rah-rah presentations, delivered with high spirits but very little substance.

As I walked away from the microphone, the crowd cheered, but I hung my head in shame. Not because I was embarrassed—and trust me, I was—but because I had let God down. He told me to sit, and I chose to stand anyhow. That day turned into an important lesson for me about the importance of being lead by the Spirit.

When I say Spirit, I'm referring to the Holy Spirit, the one God sends to dwell within us, to guide us and show us the way. We can hear the Spirit's messages so clearly as whispers to our soul. But so often we doubt what we've heard, allowing other people to convince us it isn't true.

And usually, those people don't mean us any harm. After all, they didn't hear the message meant for us. They're simply offering logical advice, so we can "get over it" and move on. That way we can quickly resume life in the way they're most familiar with relating to us.

However, **God is not in the business of helping us get over things. He seeks to make us complete.** When he allows transitions to occur in our lives, an entire metamorphosis takes place, and the things we used to do often have no place in our new normal. If they do, they serve a vastly different role.

The kicker is, often only you know it, and you struggle to articulate why you know it. Sometimes it's because you hear God's voice, and other times you have a gut feeling. It's an intuitive notion that tells you that this thing you used to do, and really liked doing, is not for you anymore.

But when we're hurt, grieving, lost or confused, we discount our ability to hear and clearly discern. It makes us susceptible to wondering if, perhaps, people around us know best. We place more confidence in their judgment than our own. As a result, we abdicate our power to make our own choices and to live our lives in the way that God is leading.

My Africa experience made clear to me that's no way to live. **I chose to get back in the driver's seat of my own life.** I didn't know exactly where I would end up, but I knew who was guiding me there. And similar to the silent ride down once our parachute opened, I decided to be obedient and enjoy the quiet until it was time to hit the ground running again.

If you're anything like me, you have moments of doubt about the messages the Spirit is whispering to you. I encourage you to meditate on this:

God has not given us a spirit of fear, but of power
and of love and of a sound mind. [4]

Don't be afraid to do what God is telling you to do. Even when it doesn't make sense to others, you can still trust His master plan. Embrace the stillness, and let the Spirit be your guide. You will never be led astray. ❣

As God leads, I will follow. As He speaks I will obey,
for the Holy Spirit lives within me, and guides my way;
I have a sound mind and a discerning spirit.
I am no longer afraid.

BOOKSHELF *boost*

Like many of you, I knew very little about grief when I was thrown into the grieving process. My transition coach recommended a valuable resource, *The Grief Recovery Handbook: The Action Program for Moving Beyond Death, Divorce and Other Losses*, by John W. James and Russell Friedman. It helped me understand the difference between getting over it and the process of getting complete, while also encouraging me to be patient with me.

Check it out at http://katrinamcghee.com/books/.

---

[4] 2 Timothy 1:7 NKJV

I Am Productive

Who do you think you are—the productivity police?

Hi, cousin.
Hey.
Did you have a good day?
Yep!
So were you productive today?
Yep! I sure was ...

I got up, took a shower, and put on some clothes. Now I was sitting on my backyard swing, journaling. Yep! That was productive.

All summer long, my cousin and I went through the same drill. She'd come home from a long day of work and school and find me barely dressed, reading, writing in my journal, or asleep.

Over and over, she'd ask me those same questions. It's as if she had become the productivity police, and I was religiously suspected of wasting time.

It drove me crazy! But I knew she was concerned that I was going through some sort of depression. After all, when I was "healthy," I had been constantly in motion. So if I was spending this much time being still, something surely had to be alarmingly wrong with me.

And she was right. There was a lot wrong with me. I was grieving and sick from exhaustion; yes, a little sad, and a lot angry, that my life was not unfolding as I had planned. Instead of easing on down the road to my next grand adventure, I was stuck in the "in between."

Have you ever been in that space? When God has told you to leave, but hasn't gotten around to sharing the details of where to go next? Man, is it frustrating! That's because busy people like us base our entire self-worth on our output. We relish the notion of checking things off our to-do list and making strides toward our goals. It leaves us with that warrior-like feeling that says I can conquer the world.

But sitting still? That drives us nuts. Things aren't getting done, and there are plenty of things in this world that could use our expertise. We simply cannot understand why God would have us sit on the sidelines instead of getting in the game.

I remember thinking surely there is more I'm supposed to be doing. But there wasn't. The only thing I'd been led to do was to start a consulting company so I could earn some money while I figured out what to do next. And thankfully, God had blessed me with a few clients right away. But the frenetic pace of my life had slowed to a crawl, and I was bored out of my mind. I was also kind of irked people wouldn't let me alone.

Now, don't get me wrong. I appreciated my friends and family's concern. It's just that over and over people would ask me the same question: 'So what are you going to do now?' And the reality is, I had no idea. No freaking clue—and that was almost worse than the boredom, because the more I said I don't know, the more I started to question if something was wrong with me.

I know many of you have experienced similar feelings with your own transitions.

> *After working as a teacher your whole adult life, you finally retire. The day after your party people start asking, "So how are you going to keep yourself busy?"*

> *You break up with your long-time boyfriend. Over drinks, your best friend tries to console you by saying, "Don't worry about it. There are plenty of other fish in the sea! Let's look around in here and see if anybody looks good."*

> *Your baby goes off to college. The day after you drop her off at school, a neighbor pops over for a visit, and the first thing they ask is, "So what are you going to do with all that free time?"*

Sure, they're just harmless questions. Mostly, people are just making conversation, not even necessarily expecting an answer. But if you're the person in transition, after a while it can get exhausting not to be able to provide an interesting or exciting response, if for no other reason than to make it seem like you're making progress.

I think this is another one of our most vulnerable places. The "in between" always lasts longer than we'd like, and the pressure we put on ourselves to move forward, coupled with the external scrutiny, can cause us to run backwards instead of waiting until it's time to take our bold step forward. Here's a picture of what that often looks like.

In the months following the organizational crisis, there was a pretty significant number of people who made career changes. By and large, I could group us into two general categories: those running away from the situation, and those moving toward a new beginning.

For those running away, it's been a bumpy road: frequent job changes, increased dissatisfaction in their new environment, and a general restlessness as they search for a place where they fit. Many have had challenges in their personal lives too, as they try to manage a highly stressful situation without the benefit of some time for reflection or the assistance of a counselor or coach. I'm always saddened when I see these smart, dynamic people hopping from place to place or staying in their new place, miserable and dissatisfied with life.

Conversely, there were those who took a bit longer. They didn't rush to find something to fill their time. They got quiet, observed the landscape, and then moved forward in a direction that made sense for where the Spirit was leading. For the most part, that group is much more content. They might not have gotten it all right, but mentally they're in a much better space because their decisions were not made out of desperation or a desire to feel good about themselves based on garnering the respect of others.

When it came time to make my choice, I soon found that, while the second option was the best route for me, it definitely wasn't easy. The temptation to move ahead before it's time comes in very attractive packaging, and encouragement to unwrap it comes from all sides.

My enticement was in the form of more job offers than I'd received in the whole of my entire life. I was incredibly grateful and flattered, but also a little baffled. I kept thinking to myself, didn't they see the firestorm I just left? Why are they calling me?

For a person who was feeling pretty bad about myself, it kind of made me feel good. It was a wonderful reminder that not everything revolved around my one bad moment in time. In fact, there were millions of people who knew nothing about it, and honestly could not care less. When they looked at my life, they saw a much broader view than my myopic mindset could embrace.

It surprised me that, in speaking with most of the recruiters, there was very little of our conversation that focused on the wildfire that just months before had felt like it would consume me. At first that excited me, until I realized that, as humbled as I was by their faith in me, I didn't really want any of those jobs. In fact, I didn't want a traditional job at all. Every time I thought about pursuing one of those positions, I heard a quiet voice say, *That's too small.*

Of course I immediately suspected I had lost my mind. These were big jobs doing important work, the kind that used to make me feel good about helping change the world. Was I crazy to let them pass me by, especially when I didn't know what I would be doing instead?

My, oh, my, how often we fall into that trap! We know deep down that something is not right for us, and yet we move forward with it anyway because we're afraid something better won't come along, or because we're tired of waiting. In our quest to move forward, we rush on down the road, only to find ourselves circling back to the very spot we were so frantically trying to leave.

Our personal lives, especially, often suffer this fate. We marry people we have doubts about, because we're lonely and don't want to be on our own anymore. Five years later, we're divorced and single yet again, only this time we bear the scars of rushing into a relationship we knew wasn't right from the get-go—all because we're desperate to have external validation for what's missing from our internal self-worth.

If we just stopped racing forward and embraced the stillness, we could avoid so much heartache. Yes, it is sometimes uncomfortable. It also can be very lonely, particularly when what God is depositing in our spirit seems so counter to what "good sense" would tell us is the right thing to do, or what our wayward hearts want to do. But if we stick with it, a short time of stillness can lead us to an incredible **moment of transcendence**.

That's when your life moves beyond the status quo into the realm of the extraordinary. You recognize it first within your spirit as a call to the beyond, and even when you don't know where you will end up, you're at peace. In fact, that is the hallmark of your transcendence—a peace that surpasses all understanding. It's one only God can give, and it is rooted in your surrender to Him.

You may not immediately experience a change in location or situation. In fact, most people I know or have read about experience their transcendence long before deliverance. That's because there must be spiritual enlightenment before there can be a physical manifestation. We are like the phoenix, whose essence is encased in the egg, lying in the ashes, being readied to take flight. Even though we're still, we are still being productive.

If you're in transition, frustrated because you can't yet see your way out, I encourage you to stand. Stay still and let God complete His work in you. Don't rush into something because you feel the need to be busy. Instead, embrace the stillness and surrender to the process. In doing so, your life will explode with possibility, ushering you into an existence you could not have hoped for or imagined.

When the waiting gets rough, repeat the phrase below. It's a great way to boost your patience and remind yourself of what's to come. ❧

Even when I'm still, I am still productive.
I can trust the process, knowing there is a divine plan.
No longer will I settle for the status quo.
I operate in the realm of the extraordinary.

BOOKSHELF *boost*

While I was in the waiting season, I started exploring my other interests. It's a great way to allow God to expose hidden talents and passions that, for whatever reason, we may have laid to the side.

For me, that was writing. As a child, I had always loved the written word. But as I grew older, I chose a career that allowed me to "make a living" using the more analytic side of my brain. As a result, I rarely had an outlet for my creative endeavors.

However, a friend recommended a book that set me free. *The Artist's Way*, by Julia Cameron, was the key to rekindling my love of creativity. Her twelve-week process is designed to discover and recover your creative self; however, for me it also set in motion a disciplined way for me to meet God in the pages of my journal every day.

Through her morning pages exercise, I was able to clear the cobwebs from my mind and focus on what was being deposited in my spirit. Eventually, those pages would lead to the birth of a new vision, and they continue to be where divine inspiration often occurs.

I encourage you to adopt journaling as an ongoing part of your life. If you've never done it before, or it's been a while, *The Artist's Way* is a great way to get back in gear.

There's a link at http://katrinamcghee.com/books/.

I Am Free

I really just needed to say it out loud.

When I was living at a manic pace, I used to wish for just a few minutes to relax and think things through. Traveling up to fifty weeks a year left very little time for reflection, let alone contemplation of meaty topics that might slow me down or sling me off track. So when I stopped racing around, all the things I had tried to run past, push to the side, or largely ignore came rushing back with a vengeance. That's when I realized why so many of us stay busy—to run away from our true selves!

All kinds of stuff bubbles to the surface that we may—or may not—want to deal with. For me, that was secrets, shame, and guilt that I had been carrying around for a long time. Things had hurt to the core, but I had powered through because, well, that's what busy women do. Even when a part of our lives is an absolute mess, we rarely stop to take a moment for self-care—that is, until we're flat on our back and can do naught else.

Suddenly, then, our physical and mental health become infinitely more important to us as we realize that, in putting everyone and everything else first, we've unconsciously moved ourselves to the sideline. Just the other week, I spoke to a friend who had ignored the warning signs of a heart attack. I was dumbstruck, until I remembered I had largely disregarded my own panic attacks, which I thought were a heart attack and stroke combined.

But I've learned that you can't cheat nature. Eventually, when you least expect or desire it, life will remind you what you've left undone. It's at that point you begin reconciling with your true self and letting everything that doesn't fit fall to the wayside.

I liken it to the process of unpacking an old backpack. You know, sometimes when we're getting ready to go on a trip, we pull out our backpack only to find there are things we left inside. Some of it is still good and we leave alone, while other stuff we immediately discard. It's spoiled, we've outgrown it, or it's no longer useful in our lives.

Then there's the pile of stuff that needs special attention. We have to study it before we can decide what to do with it. We know we should have done something with it a long time ago, but for whatever reason, we couldn't ever seem to get around to it.

I had more of those than I cared to acknowledge. Seemed like the more I searched for the next step I was to take, the more these unresolved issues appeared. It was as if God was saying, *You've got to deal with this before we can go on to the next season.*

Three things in particular kept coming back around—my abortion, my brief marriage, and my search for my biological father. Now, I'm sure some folks have been stunned into silence and probably have dropped the book. I'll pause for a moment while you compose yourself. Gratefully, the shock has passed for me.

The shock of talking about it, that is. Because, had you asked me just a few years ago, I would have told you I'm taking my thoughts on all of these to the grave. The shame and embarrassment factors alone were enough to ensure my silence, but it was honestly my carefully crafted persona that kept my lips sealed. After all, what would people think of me if they knew?

That's where I had put my energy all those years—wondering what people would think. What I should have been questioning is what does God think of me, and how do I feel about me? Had I done that, I would have healed much quicker.

Certainly that was the case for the abortion I had when I was seventeen. Back then, I was a kid living a thousand miles away from home, had just discovered sex, and was a bit of a wild child. I was so young, and when I got pregnant I just wanted to make it go away. On the day of the abortion, I remember being a little sad, but mostly relieved. Now, no one would have to know of my colossal mistake. After all, I was a good Christian girl who came from a great family. What would people think?

It wasn't until years later, when I had to have a hysterectomy, that the repercussions of my decision became clear. By then I was already blessed to have had a child, but the reality of never being able to bear another hit me like a ton of bricks. Never had I regretted a decision more, but there was no undoing it. The grief over the life I had so carelessly tossed aside was a palpable thing.

I judged the young girl I was so harshly, frustrated over my naïve behavior and shortsightedness. But as angry as I was, I didn't dwell there too long. In fact, I didn't even really acknowledge my grief—not even to me. I just kept rolling along, too ashamed to discuss it.

Years later I handled the demise of my marriage much the same way. We were only married for a few years, but I felt like I aged about fifty. The constant yelling and bickering was not what I had anticipated during our whirlwind courtship and engagement. I couldn't believe a "smart woman like me" had fallen for the old bait and switch. But there I was, married to a man I barely knew, and afraid he would erupt at any moment.

Of course I couldn't tell anyone. I was an executive, well respected, and known as a strong advocate for women. No one could find out my child and I were living in hell at home. How could I explain how I had gotten myself into such a mess?

Through the grace of God, my son and I were able to escape and slowly rebuild our lives. But I noticed that even with counseling, I was left with a residue of anger that I couldn't shake. It wasn't just directed at my ex-husband. I was mad at me too, especially for putting my son in such a turbulent situation. I kept asking myself what good mother would do such a thing? Ironically, it was the search for my own biological parent that helped me put it all in perspective.

You see, my mom and dad married when I was four years old. I remember at their wedding running up to my dad to confirm that I could now call him "Daddy." It was a special moment that left everyone smiling as they watched our little family come to life.

Soon after, we moved across country, and I was legally adopted. Most people had no idea that Dad wasn't my biological father, including me. It wasn't until I was a bit older that my parents explained our situation. They wanted to make sure when I found out, I heard it from them, not someone back home who knew but didn't realize I didn't know. I honestly don't even remember our conversation. What I most recall is being desperate to keep my secret.

From the moment I found out there was a part of me someplace else, I felt an unexplainable separation, as if a piece of me had come untethered from my family. They treated me just the same, but inside, things had changed. At times, I felt like an odd man out, because there were little things about myself I couldn't explain.

Simple stuff, like people asking me where I got my hazel eyes, became a big deal to me. No one else in my immediate family had them, so I assumed they came from my unknown biological. But every time someone inquired, I was always careful not to in any way indicate I wasn't a full-fledged member of my family. In my mind, I needed to keep my secret so I could belong.

It wasn't until I was an adult and a mom myself that I became somewhat comfortable sharing my secret. By then I knew my biological father's name and had made up my mind I would one day find him. It wasn't because I felt like our family was missing anything. I just wanted to find the rest of me.

My summer of stillness, when God was reconciling all of me back to Him, seemed the right time to pursue my goal. Amazingly, it wasn't too difficult to locate him. Turns out, his last known address was an assisted living center which was about a five-hour drive from my home.

I suppose I should have called first, but I was afraid of being rejected over the phone. I just decided, it's time and I'm going for it. So one morning a friend and I set out to spend a couple of days in my biological father's hometown, thinking we'd just pop in and say hello.

Well, that bold courage went scurrying away the minute it was time for us to head over to see him. When we pulled up, I had to be helped out of the car. My fear had increased about 1,000 percent. Walking to the front door felt like I was playing out a scene from the movie *The Green Mile*, in which prisoners would yell out "dead man walking" as their fellow inmates took their final steps to the electric chair.

I honestly had no idea what to expect. My heart was beating so fast it's a wonder I didn't faint. But as it turns out, this visit would be a bust. Not only did he not live there, they'd never even heard of him!

A couple of hours later, after calling around to his old neighbors, we found out he had already passed away. I was a little sad and thought perhaps that was the end of my journey. But a few minutes later, the phone rang. It was a gentleman who had been mentored by my biological father. Evidently the old couple we'd called had called him, and he was phoning to see if he could be of assistance.

Actually, I'm pretty sure it was curiosity, along with his helpful spirit, that compelled him to pick up the phone. After all, it was a small country place and everybody knew everybody. An unknown relative showing up out of nowhere must have been the talk of the town.

We chit-chatted for a bit, getting to know each other, before he finally got around to asking me how he could help. And in the blink of an eye, I froze. The fear and shame came rushing forward, choking off my words. What if he didn't believe me? What if I found out things I didn't want to know?

That's what fear and shame do to us. They lock us inside a world of "what ifs" and "what will I dos." We prewrite our story, and as a result, we miss out on what is and what could be. I decided, not this time. I was already too late to meet him. I might as well try and find out as much about him as I could. So, I laid it all out to see what response I'd get. "Sir, forty-four years ago my mom and your mentor had a brief relationship. I am the result of their time together. I decided after four decades that it was time to come find my father. I'm hoping you can tell me a bit about him."

"Woooooooooow!" I think it took him a full sixty seconds to get that one word out. But then he blew me away with his kindness. He said, "Well, I'm sorry you didn't get a chance to meet him, because he was a good man. If you'd like, I can e-mail you a copy of his funeral program. It has a lot of information about him I think you'd find interesting."

He was so right. Reading the program, I found the missing pieces of myself. We were similar in appearance, had the same college degrees, and lo and behold, he had even been a writer. I finally felt whole and, to my great surprise, free.

Turns out, I didn't need to meet him as much as I just needed to accept who I was and have the courage to say it out loud. Of course it would have been wonderful to see him face to face and have time to truly get to know him. But the great gift of the whole experience was that I was finally able to release myself from the secret I had held so dear, and the shame of being born on the wrong side of the marriage ceremony. At long last, I was free to just be me.

On the way back home, my friend asked me how I felt about my mom. He wondered if I was angry with her for not allowing me to meet my biological father when I was young. I thought about it for a moment, and I realized there was no anger in me— at either of my parents. Why would there be, when I was raised in a loving household where my mom and dad did everything humanly possible to care for me and make the best decisions they could for my future?

Was our house perfect? No. But my experience raising my own child helped me understand that parenting and perfection are almost never used in the same sentence. Most of us are doing the best we can with what we have, and we have to trust it is enough.

It was days later when that very notion made me stop and rethink the judgment I had been harboring of myself: the disappointment in the young girl who chose to have an abortion, and the irritation in the thirty-something woman who fell in love and married the wrong guy. Why was I so hard on the younger me when I could so easily give others the benefit of the doubt?

I thought about it for quite a while and finally came to the conclusion that there was no good reason for me not to forgive me. I had already asked God for forgiveness long ago. It was time for me to accept it and move ahead. Just like my parents, I was making the best decisions I knew how. Did I make some mistakes? Yes. But it was time I made peace with my past. After all, I was still God's masterpiece, and He loved me no matter what.

How freeing it was to finally let go of the shame and self-judgment! It was as if a weight I never knew existed had been taken off my back, and I could finally stand tall. But you know the interesting thing is, as I prepared to write this book, I still struggled with whether to include this chapter. After all, even if I'm okay with my past, it doesn't mean others will be as forgiving. I'm sure there will be people reading this who think less of me and wonder if I'm truly okay with having never met my biological father, or if I'm secretly upset with my parents and just won't say.

But I've decided if I can help just one person experience the euphoria of freedom, then the possibility of others judging me is worth the risk. It's worth it because I meet so many women who are doing the same thing I was doing—beating themselves up over what happened in the past. We say things like:

I was so stupid back then. If only I could do things over again.

I can't believe I fell for his lies. I should have known better.

What was I thinking? How could I have made such a dumb decision?

We repeat it over and over, trying to make sense of things we regret, because the person we are now can't remotely comprehend what the person we were before was thinking. But the reality is that no understanding will ever come from berating ourselves. Instead, we learn not to trust our own judgment, letting fear of failure handicap our growth and development in critical areas of our life.

We have to remember *the powerful lens of hindsight was never designed to make us feel bad about our past. It was given so that we have a better future.* The only real way for us to move forward without our past weighing us down is to leave guilt, shame, and self-judgment behind.

Believe me, I know it's easier said than done. There are some things that many of us deeply regret. But no matter what you have done, what you feel ashamed of, or what other people have told you about what you did, there's something I want you to know.

*If you ask, God will forgive. There is nothing you can do that will ever separate you from His love. When you accept that as truth, you can forgive you too, because there will be no doubt that **you are worthy of your own love and respect.***

Reaffirming our worth based on who God created us to be gives us the courage to move beyond our past. It's then that we can go ahead and unpack our backpacks so that secrets, guilt, and shame no longer weigh us down.

Let's start by taking out all that old stuff we've been carrying around that we've never made peace with and gently begin the process of letting go. Don't pull it out and set about judging you, and don't put yourself on a deadline. Instead, be kind and remind yourself that healing takes time.

What's the first step in our restoration? Replacing the negative thoughts that feed our shame with encouraging words that affirm our value. Every time you start to beat yourself up, I want you to say the words below. In time, your beliefs about you will change, and your life will take on new meaning. ❧

I am God's masterpiece—a one-of-a-kind unique design.
Nothing I do will ever separate me from His love.
When I ask, He forgives and sets me free.
From this day forward, I love me, I accept me, I forgive me.

BOOKSHELF *boost*

Accepting God's forgiveness frees us to move on, forgiving ourselves and others. But exercising that freedom takes work, often taking years before we're brave enough to put it into action. That's why I recommend *Let it Go*, by T.D. Jakes. In it, he explores the concept of forgiveness and gives practical advice on how to apply it to your daily life.

If you're struggling to see how you can possibly let go of the past, I highly recommend you pick up a copy. There is no greater gift you can give yourself than the freedom to leave the past behind.

You can find a link on my bookshelf at http://katrinamcghee. com/books/.

I Am Valuable

You want me to do what? I'm not qualified for that.

One of the great benefits of dealing with the unaddressed issues of our past is that it clears up mental space in the present. It allows the whole of ourselves to focus on what's before us, viewing life through a broader lens of possibility rather than pessimism, confusion, and defeat. It's from this vantage point that we are best poised to explore life beyond our comfort zone.

After a few months of rest and reflection, I felt that shift happen for me. It was as if the fog surrounding my brain slowly began to recede, allowing my mind to fill with random thoughts and ideas. I couldn't put it all together yet, but it felt like glimpses of the future.

Looking back, I see how God was taking me through a process of reshaping my thinking before he'd allow me to take those first steps. Bit by bit, spending time with Him evolved my beliefs about who I am and who He is. Knowing my true self, defining my worth based on who He created me to be, and accepting this one truth greatly expanded the prospects for my life:

I am because He is, and because He is, anything is possible.

Believing this meant I didn't have to be confined by what I had been or knew how to do. I could be whoever He wanted me to be, and I could know that whatever He asked me to do, it would be enough. *But what was it?*

Journaling was the best way for me to get quiet enough to hear God's answers. Through daily writing, I was able to slow down my constantly racing thoughts and drop into a space where it was He and me alone. It was there where my imagination took flight in a more cohesive manner.

Soon a cornucopia of ideas—both new and dusted-off old ones—emerged. My transition coach called it a creative tornado, but for me it felt like I was finally alive again, awake and ready to reengage with the world. What got me especially excited was a concept for a new women's community. I referred to it as *Do Good Girlz*, a place where young women could connect their passion with their true purpose.

My idea was to get someone to write a program that would serve as the "brain" for our website, the goal being to use technology to match a woman's unique gifts, talents, values, and resources with a variety of causes and organizations that, based on her responses, would be of interest. After completing our survey, each "Do Good Girl" would receive a unique plan to put her passions into action, and together we would change the world.

It sounded so wonderful, marrying all my loves—mentoring young women, creating communities, and supporting great causes. It also met a need. For years, young women had been asking me, "How do I know what I'm supposed to be doing? How do I take what I'm good at and help other people?" Well, here was the solution! *Do Good Girlz* would revolutionize the way women engaged in supporting local and global communities.

The best part was this was a natural next step for what I had been doing all my life, what I was good at. So I started getting all my ducks in a row. I secured the website, graphic designer, and a project manager. I even put together a small focus group and started meeting with them regularly to test out my ideas.

There was just one problem—they didn't get it. What seemed so obvious on paper fell flat in the telling. They kept asking me hard questions like, "What's the goal? What are you trying to achieve? Why would women engage, and why would they come back after the first time?" My answer was always, "Let me think about that." What I really wanted to say was, "Look, this is an inspiration from God. Just go with it!"

But my gut was telling me they were right. There was something missing. It felt incomplete, like I had snatched up a piece and tried to make it the whole picture. You know how we do, so eager to get started we hear a smidgen of something and then take off running like we know the whole story, only to have to stop a few steps later to get the rest of what we need.

That's what I ended up doing, going back to the journal to ask God what I was missing. And that's when He started showering me with additional pieces to the puzzle.

> *It's a movement, about women for women.*
> *It's built on the spirit of abundance.*
> *It's a partnership and a platform.*

It's where inspiration meets opportunity.
It's about choices that change our world.
It's a blog. It's a business. It's a community.
It's a place of healing and restoration.

Honestly, I felt a little all over the place and yet still on the right path. Although "it" didn't completely sync up with my original idea for *Do Good Girlz*, it totally lined up with this leg of my journey. Even the affirmations I scribbled in the margins of my journal were reflections of what God was teaching me about me.

I can change the world.
I was created for a unique purpose, something only I can do.
I care about myself, my village, and my world.
I am mighty. I am strong. I am enough.
I choose to do good!

It seemed this message of being enough, which was so central to my own healing, was at the core of what God was asking me to share with the world. Whereas I had latched on to the "do" part, God backed me up once again to "be."

It's funny how even after God delivers us, we run back to our comfort zone. It's that safe place where we know we can excel and be accepted and respected. But what we find out quickly is that it's no longer enough. God has expanded our thinking and given us a yearning to grow that can only be satisfied when we surrender to His plan.

Of course we don't always recognize what's happening in the moment. All we know is that what used to thrill us, what seemed so perfect for us before, now is inadequate to fulfill the longing in the depths of our soul. So we're faced with a choice—do we continue what we're doing, in spite of the warnings, until another life-interrupted moment occurs, or do we take a leap of faith into the unknown?

It's our choice. Really, it is. We can choose to see ourselves as God sees us, and trust He has a better plan. Or we can trust we know best and stay stuck in the status quo. The choice is ours, but so are the consequences.

Rather than continuing down a path which wasn't coming together, I decided to go with God and see where He led. I took my plans I had fallen in love with and placed them to the side, and instead picked up my random puzzle pieces to see what other options would take shape. And you know what? An amazing thing occurred. God took what I already had and gave me a whole new plan.

It was an intimate conversation with Him in the pages of my journal where my new path was revealed. I started with the same basic question: "God, what is it you would have me do?" Then I began listing all the pieces of the puzzle He had placed in my heart, the things I knew with certainty in the depths of my soul. Two pages in, here's an excerpt from my journal where His plans for me began to unfold:

> *You have asked me to be a light. To let your love shine through. To be an encourager—especially to young women, but in truth us all. I want this to be "Our Spot." The place where women go to get inspiration, encouragement, and a challenging word ... a place to plan, vent, be inspired, and just share good girl talk. We're not experts, just women who want to live in the spirit of abundance. Father, please help me think of a title. Something unique—unlike others but that resonates and rejuvenates. That means something personal to me and to countless other women who*

need encouragement—a meditation to carry them
through. It's not common, but it's simple—Loving
on Me! Oh, thank you God. It covers every area. So
simple and yet so empowering ...

And just like that, the pieces began falling into place. God had taken my mess and given me a message for the world. A quick search of the Web revealed that not only was the Website available, but every social medium was too. Everything I needed was already in place. *Loving on Me* had been made ready and was waiting for me all along.

Less than three weeks after my conversation with God, I launched the blog, and the next phase of my life was born. It wasn't what I had planned, but it was clearly His. Honestly, I was shocked at how we were able to do the logo design, web development, and writing so quickly. But a girlfriend of mine shared a bit of wisdom from one of her mentors that helped put things in perspective—*Be prepared for suddenly.*

She said that's how God works. We toil, we wait, we pace and pray, and then all at once things come together and we see the beginnings of what God was planning all along. It appears as if it suddenly came into being, only when we think on it, we can see how He's been preparing us throughout our journey. We just rarely get there along the path we anticipate.

It's why so many of us stay stuck and frustrated for so long. We fall in love with our plans, and they slowly begin to impede our progress. But of course we don't see it that way, because they're great plans! Why wouldn't they work? They've worked for other people, they follow the natural progression of things, and they make sense. We couldn't possibly imagine that God could have a whole different agenda ... especially one that's outside of our comfort zone.

Which is exactly where *Loving on Me* turned out to be. You see, *Do Good Girlz* was where I felt at home. I knew about doing good and supporting great causes. After all, I was a nonprofit "professional." I had worked in the field for twenty years and had education to support my experience.

But this business of loving myself and living abundantly? I was still figuring that out. Who was I to offer advice, and more importantly, why would anyone listen? I had no degree in psychology, no certification, no training in coaching … just nothing. I felt completely unqualified and yet totally called.

Can I tell you I drove myself crazy with this round-the-way thinking those first few months I was writing the blog? I kept wondering when I would run out of things to talk about, or when someone was going to call me on my lack of credentials. Often it would take me days to get a blog "just right," terrified that I would be immortalized as an idiot in the written word.

Finally, I realized people weren't really looking for me to be profound as much as they needed me to be authentic. And that's what God was asking me to do—be myself and encourage others to do the same. He wants me to transparently share my struggle so we can all learn the lessons and move to higher ground, together.

I genuinely believe **God uses us best outside of our comfort zone**—not outside of the gifts and talents He's blessed us with, but outside of the box in which we've so neatly placed them. In that space, we are totally dependent on Him for direction, not on our own finite thinking and abilities.

Everything we need, He has a plan to provide. For example, the advice I felt unqualified to share? I found it in the lessons from my own experience and in the myriad of stories shared by other women on the blog. The solutions to our everyday challenges? I found in God's word and in the many books I read, written by people further down the path. I discovered I didn't have to know everything to be ready. I just had to be open, willing, and obedient. He'd take care of the rest.

So my question for you is, what's holding you back? Have you fallen in love with your plans so much that they're holding you in place? Or maybe you're afraid of moving forward because you don't yet know all the steps? Whatever it is, I encourage you to take a deep breath, and move on anyhow.

Don't let fear of the unknown rob you of your future. Let go of what you think has to be. Just be where you are, believe what God has said about you, and trust that whatever he's given you right now is enough to get started. I am a living witness that even when it doesn't turn out like you plan, it can still be perfect for you. After all … you're reading *Loving on Me*, right?

If you don't take anything else away from this chapter know this: There is something just beyond your comfort zone that God is preparing especially for you. It may not come in the packaging you expect, or at the point in time you think is right, but when it comes, you will know it's your right path.

Don't settle for less than what He designed for you. Love yourself enough to wait on your above-and-beyond outside-the-box life. If He hasn't revealed it to you yet, be patient. You want His best, instead of later having to ask Him to bless your mess.

If you really want a life beyond your wildest dreams, start with the prayer below, and then watch Him work. I don't know a single person who has lived to regret it. ❦

> *God, thy will be done. What is it you would have me to do? Whatever it is, I'm ready and willing.*

BOOKSHELF *boost*

Stepping outside your comfort zone can be a little scary! But if you trust God, He will give you the courage to move forward, along with the experience of a lifetime. Need a little inspiration? Check out *If You Want to Walk On Water, You've Got to Get Out of the Boat,* by John Ortberg.

The central character is Peter, who was the only soul brave enough to ask for, and receive, the adventure of walking on water with Jesus. It's a perfect reminder that with God, all things are possible.

Get your copy at: http://katrinamcghee.com/books/.

I Am On Time

Why can't I write this stupid book?

Timing is a difficult thing to master, because rarely are we and God on the same timetable. We think we are, but then our plans seem to slow down or stagnate, causing us to realize that maybe we don't quite have the whole picture yet. Which brings us to another decision point; do we rush ahead, or do we wait? Our choice in this moment often determines how rocky our road becomes. This is a lesson I, unfortunately, have had to learn more than once, beginning a few months after the blog launched and I started trying to write a book.

Wanting to become an author wasn't a total surprise for me, given I've always had a love affair with the written word. One of my favorite childhood memories is spending Saturday afternoons at the bookstore with my dad. Even as a kid, I could see myself some day adding a title or two to the shelves.

But honestly, I didn't start writing the book to fulfill a lifelong dream. I did it because I was ready to turn a corner. You see, I didn't want to be a consultant for long. That felt too much like doing the same thing I'd been doing—only with less benefits and bravado. I was impatient to break out and begin my new life as a respected author, entrepreneur, and motivational speaker.

Sounds impressive, right? I could see it so clearly, traveling the world speaking and signing books. It was going to be amazing! Never mind that I had never tried to write a book before, or that I had no idea how to even begin. I had visualized it, I believed it, and I was confident it was all going to come together.

But the book I set out to write is not the book you're holding. It was another one I had had an idea for years earlier, comprised of lessons learned from behind the closed door. These were the things your bosses discussed in private meetings, but almost never said directly to you. I'd been speaking on the subject for years, and young professionals always found it helpful. So I thought, since I already had the outline, this was a good place to start.

Now I know you must be wondering why I didn't write about *Loving on Me*. After all, wasn't that where God had directed my focus? Well, yes, it was, but there were two problems with writing that book. First, I didn't know nearly enough about the topic to fill a book. I was still learning myself. Second, I didn't want to get pigeonholed into only doing one thing. Katrina McGhee was so much more than just *Loving on Me*.

Don't get me wrong. I loved this journey of learning to love myself more. It had brought me closer to God than I had ever been in my entire life. But I wanted to embrace the business side of myself too, because, let's be honest—that's where my years of experience and expertise (also known as my credibility) was based.

In my mind, if I wanted people to listen to anything I had to say, I needed to begin where I had left off.

So, I slowly started working on my career book. Trouble is, I could never get in a rhythm. I assumed it was a lack of time. After all, my consulting practice was growing, and I was on the road a lot more. I figured maybe I just need to focus, take some time away, and do nothing but write. So for three weeks in December I went to the mountains. This was going to be my writing retreat. I just knew when I left I'd have a finished manuscript.

Needless to say I was wrong, wrong, wrong. Forget a finished manuscript—I couldn't write a single word. Every time I sat down to work on the book, I'd get super sleepy and have to go lie down. It was both funny and frustrating, as over and over again God said no.

I realize now that trying to write a business book was nothing but me running from the life He was calling me to live. Scared of losing the old me, I kept trying to latch on to the credibility of my past as a pathway to my future. But in the end that never works. **What was before prepares us for what will be. However, if we want to move forward, we've got to let go and be willing to take a leap of faith.** Embracing the unknown, and releasing preconceived notions of what we'll do when we get there, is part of the journey.

This was tough for me because I was still trying to find some way to fully describe my new career. Consultant seemed too blah—especially when I compared it to my old title. I didn't want to be just a blogger either. I knew *Loving on Me* was way more than that. So what was it I was supposed to tell people I was doing? What is the best way to describe ourselves when there doesn't seem to be a word that quite fits?

Obviously, God knew I would reach this place. One of the last things I threw in my suitcase was a copy of Tama Kieves' *Inspired and Unstoppable.* That book spoke to my spirit in a way nothing else had. She was a person who had been where I was, understood my struggles, and was wildly cheering me on from the sidelines.

Through her experiences I could see how walking an inspired path leads to leaving our old yardstick for success behind. It also necessitates letting go of our hard and fast plans of what comes next and just working with what's in front of us. For me, that meant no way could I reach back and grab my old outline for a new message. If I was to write a book, it needed to be about *Loving on Me*.

But how could I when I wasn't ready? Even though I was writing blogs, I still didn't feel like I had enough to share in book format. I'm sure that's partly because I didn't want to write one of those dinky self-help books that looked like it came out of someone's outdated typewriter. Of course I could do that, but I had higher standards.

Yeah, right. Ego is a deceitful rascal. Have you noticed how it gives us the illusion of excellence while locking us in a cycle of mediocrity? Instead of focusing on being our best self, ego drives us to want to be better than somebody else. So as a result, we let what we perceive we lack guide our way, rather than maximizing our strengths and seeing where they lead us.

That's why I spent the next fifteen months in and out of classes, workshops, and seminars. Determined to educate myself about what women really needed, my first stop was a global women's summit. The keynote speakers were all at the top of their game, and their presentations were outstanding. However, it was the Q&A that followed that was the most enlightening for me.

It seemed no matter what subject we were discussing, the questions always circled back to the same thing—how do I choose me? Not can I change my life, but *how* do I do it? What gave you the courage to take the first step?

People didn't want theories. They wanted practical advice, and more importantly, they were hungry for stories of transformation.

Not just the pretty results where you're beautifully in bloom on the other side, but the raw, unfiltered process of going from where they are to where God was calling them to be.

One woman in particular really struck a chord with me. She asked the question, "What do you do when the shoes you're wearing are too small?" I could hear the frustration in her voice as her soul was yearning to break free from the confines of her narrow existence. But she had no idea how.

The speakers—who were both incredibly accomplished—responded to her from their current season in life. It was great advice, but it was too advanced for her situation. She needed the first step, just so she could take a deep breath.

My heart went out to her, and I couldn't help but raise my hand. When one of the speakers called on me, I thanked them for sharing, told them how inspiring I thought they were, and then I turned to the sister who was hurting and said something like this:

> *When the shoes you're wearing are too small, you must take them off. No one will do it for you. You have the power to take that one step, and when you do, God will show you what's next. You'll never find out which shoes do fit if you keep your toes cramped up in the ones that don't. Because forcing yourself into something too small always focuses your energy on your pain, rather than your infinite possibilities.*

The room erupted in applause, and many women came up to hug me after. What was interesting to me is that I didn't think I had done anything spectacular. I just shared one of the lessons from my own journey, which at the end of the day, turned out to be enough.

So if that's all I really needed to do to encourage others why was I struggling to write this stupid book? It was stupid because I was stumped, and by now frustrated because I couldn't figure out what was wrong. In listening to speaker after speaker talk about things that I'd already written about over the last year it seemed clear—the book was in the blogs. There was nothing I needed that God hadn't already given me or would give me in the future. So what was stopping me? Was it my writing skills?

After all, writing a book was surely different than a blog. Maybe I needed to better understand the mechanics to get myself in gear. So I signed up for a writer's conference, with the goal of turning thousands of words I'd written on the blog into a book. Or at the very least, to figure out what was holding me back.

That ten days away turned out to be just what I needed. The conference rekindled my joy in writing and connected me with my new tribe. Every day I was surrounded by people who shared the same loves as I did. We got each other—and in a weird way became an eclectic and merry band of travelers, creating our own sweet melody as we shared encouragement and critiques.

Being with them reminded me of the gift, and power, of community, because who we surround ourselves with in large part dictates who we become, and yet, we often put very little effort in consciously choosing our community. Instead, most of us go with the flow, meeting whom we meet and allowing them to take a seat.

But I'm of a different mindset these days. I choose to fill my life with positive people who uplift, affirm, and inspire. I want to be surrounded by people who lead with love and are willing to accept the same. Are they perfect? Heck, no! They'd never be able to tolerate me if they were. But together, we are a wonderful blend of the diversity and magnificence of God's creation. We sharpen and shape each other, together growing in grace.

The writing group definitely did that for me. Our collective creative energy quickly propelled me forward. By the middle of the week I had an outline, introduction, and the first chapter complete. I was rocking and rolling right up until I had to read aloud those first few pages to my classmates. That's when something strange happened. Out of nowhere, I got angry.

Just reading aloud the portion about the panic attacks was darn near causing me to have another one. I couldn't believe it. How was it that over a year later, I hadn't gotten beyond the hurt and anger? Would I ever be back to normal again?

As my classmates began sharing their feedback I became more and more upset. They were looking for details, salacious tidbits about why the organization had gone into crisis and who was to blame. They said the story needed more drama in order to draw people in. But I knew in my spirit that this was a book about deliverance and transformation. I wasn't called to create some sort of hyped-up written reality show. I wanted to help women improve their own reality.

So I decided to take a pause—unwilling to write what they wanted and unable to write what I knew it should be, at least right now. Obviously, I needed more time to heal. And I knew that if I ignored what the Spirit was telling me, whatever I created was going to be another hot mess talking about all kinds of things I had no business talking about, all to satisfy my ego rather than my divine call.

That's why we have to be so careful to be in tune with God's timing, rather than our own desire to rush ahead. It's a tricky thing, because our ego will have us believe that we can "make it happen," assuming that everything we don't accomplish is because of something we lack, or some solution we have yet to uncover.

But sometimes it's God who hits the brakes. He says no, or not now. We may not understand it, or in anger accept it, but one thing is certain—when we go against His timing, we never achieve our highest and best. Instead, we often find ourselves in an endless pattern of repeating our mistakes, or worse yet, being hurt over and over as we try to force our way ahead.

If God is pumping the brakes in an area of your life, I encourage you to stop. Don't fall into the ego's trap of feeling like a failure when things don't go according to your plans. Instead, trust in His divine timing, knowing He has the master plan. When it's the right time, you won't have to force it.

Listen, I don't want to act like this is easy. Like most of you, I can get frustrated when God's timing is not on the same internal timetable I have for success. But when I realize I am trying my best and things still aren't coming together, I intentionally take a pause and consult Him.

My experience has been that one of three things happens. If I'm to move ahead, He reorders my steps so it's clear what's next. However, sometimes I'm working on the wrong thing entirely. In that case, he redirects me to a different path, placing my energy where He's already working. And then other times, He just has me wait.

How do I know which one it is? By focusing on what's right in front of me. I can't look at the future and always know what's next. But if I look at what God has given me this day—what need He's placed in front of me to address, what opportunity He's given me to explore, or what problem He's given me the wisdom to solve—then I know where to work.

As you can imagine, it's not always where I would have chosen to spend my time. For example, my goal was to have finished the book you're reading almost three years earlier than when it was eventually published. But had I, it wouldn't be as honest as it is today, because the courage to share intimate parts of my heart emerged as I have faced new challenges along my journey.

That's why I encourage you, above all else to seek Him. I can't say for sure what God's plan is for you, but I know with certainty that His desire is never for us to waste our time, talent, or treasure. If you don't know what to do next, if you feel like you're running in circles or facing what seem like insurmountable roadblocks, take a pause and talk to Him.

Here's a short prayer to get you started. I encourage you to write it at the top of one of the pages in your journal, and then start listening. Write down notes of what you see around you, what you *can* do right now, and what He's depositing in your spirit as your role in the here and now. Don't worry, you won't fall behind. He's got the future covered too! ❦

> God, I don't want to run ahead or lag behind.
> Keep me in lock-step with you, working on what
> you have for me to focus on this day. Amen

BOOKSHELF *boost*

I highly recommend picking up *Inspired and Unstoppable*. Reading Tama's book is like meeting an old friend who has been waiting on you to join her on the journey all along. I especially encourage those of you who may be struggling with trying to hold on to the "credibility" of your old life, while embracing God's calling.

Tama will make you feel right at home on this wild and wacky new adventure. Be sure to drop me a line to let me know what nuggets you take away from experiencing her brand of magic. It would be great if you'd drop her one too!

Check my bookshelf at http://katrinamcghee.com/books/ to pick up your copy.

LESSON NINE

I Am Growing

I can't believe she's more popular than me!

S uccess is another tricky little monster. We're all hardwired to pursue it, but our definition of achieving it is vastly different. For some, it's the accumulation of wealth, while others strive for power, respect, or fame. For me, it's always been making a difference. Since I was a little kid, I've wanted to change the world.

I'm not talking about tiny improvements that make life sweeter. I mean big sweeping changes that revolutionize the way people live. My greatest thrill is starting with an idea and building something magical. And if I'm really clicking along, I'm creating multiple things at the same time.

This explains why, as I was trying to write the book, I was simultaneously forming companies. I already had a growing consulting company, and then came *Loving on Me*. I parked a third concept to pursue later, and had another idea waiting in the wings. I know it sounds crazy, but that's how my mind works. On any given day I can have twenty to thirty ideas running through my head. The challenge has always been to figure out what's worth pursuing and when, especially in this season when I felt as though I had an overabundance of time on my hands

To sort it all out, I sat down with one of my mentors. She listened intently as I walked through how I thought all my ideas would work in sync. My plan was fairly simple. Consulting would serve as my temporary base, giving me steady income. *Loving on Me* would continue growing as a movement, with the goal of launching an affirmation-based product line to support my philanthropic efforts. The other two businesses would launch over the next eighteen months, providing residual income for my future. All the while, I'd be writing books and speaking as well.

Whew! I'm exhausted just thinking about it. Why in the world did I feel like I needed to do everything all at once? Oh yeah ... because once I got started, I went right back to my old pattern of being busy. Not content to just work the field God had already given me, I had to go buy up a couple of others—just to make sure I had enough to do, and the resources to keep doing it for the long haul.

Of course things didn't quite roll out as planned. It's been three years since my mentor and I chatted, and I'm still consulting—not to mention just getting around to finishing my first book. All I can say is thank God for wise counselors, who save us from ourselves.

After listening to my spiel, my mentor asked a few questions, gave me some counsel on consulting, and didn't say much else. Instead she called me *early* the next morning and said, "I prayed for you, and God told me to tell you that the key to your success is *Loving on Me.* Focus your energy there, and everything else will flow from it. Just be patient, continue consulting so you'll have some income, and let things evolve. Put all your other plans on the back burner."

Wow! What an incredible gift of love it was for this busy woman to take the time to pray for me. Not only did her words ring true, but the way in which she delivered them also taught me a valuable lesson about mentoring. She didn't just give me advice based solely on her experience and expertise. Instead, she was wise enough to seek God's will in what He would have her say to me, and then she spoke those words into my spirit.

And I knew she was right. It was a message from God's heart straight to my own, with the smartness of it resonating deep within my soul. It confirmed what I sensed He had been saying to me privately, but for whatever reason I struggled to accept— *Loving on Me* is enough. This vision of a women's movement, one that allows us to be who we are created to be, was to be my priority. Trouble is, I had no idea how to do it.

That's the thing about visions—as exciting as they are, they don't come with instruction manuals. Instead, God gives us three basic commands:

- Believe what I have shown you.
- Trust me to give you everything you need.
- Follow my instructions as they appear.

Now that we've walked a ways together, you can probably guess that whole "as they appear" was a challenge for me. I was ready to go to work, and I wanted to do more than just write. So I decided, rather than wait for more instructions, I'd get cracking on what I thought I knew how to do. I focused my energy on building the brand. My first order of business: increase visitors and views for the blog.

I set myself a goal of five thousand views per month. It wasn't much, but it seemed like a respectable amount for the first year. To achieve it, I started posting more often, usually two or three times a week. I also launched a couple of social media communities and a newsletter. I even hired a firm to make sure our posts reached a global audience. For months on end, I would wake up and ask myself *What can I do today to reach more people?*

At first, I would get so excited every time someone new would join our small tribe. When a person commented or shared a post, I would quickly respond so they'd know how grateful I was for their support. In those early days, little things meant a lot.

But the bigger our tribe became, the more I found myself obsessively checking the numbers instead of acknowledging with gratitude our progress. For a time, my entire focus for *Loving on Me* was consumed with how to increase page views, social media followers, and newsletter subscribers. These became my barometers for success.

Regularly, I would tweak my approach to see if I could mimic what I saw as the rapid growth of other brands. By the time our first anniversary rolled around, I had redesigned the website, rewritten the site content, and employed dozens of marketing tactics, all to increase our monthly reach. I was determined to show that this passion God had placed in the depths of my soul had a purpose, and it mattered.

That was the issue, you see. I needed *Loving on Me* to be a success to show I'd made the right choice, that walking this non-traditional path, refusing to take a job, and pouring tons of money into a vision that was not making one red cent made sense. I was trying to validate my leap of faith by landing well and easily sliding into my next adventure.

Sound familiar? I bet some of you who have started your own businesses or ministries can relate. We start out on fire for the mission. But our joy in the little things quickly disintegrates as we doggedly pursue an acceptable level of success that others can appreciate, one that will make us stand out in the crowd or set us apart in a way that gives us a unique level of credibility with the people around us.

We want to be impressive, and we will work ourselves into the ground to get there. But you know what? As hard as I tried, nothing seemed to accelerate the growth process. Sure, the tribe was increasing a little each month, but it felt too small to consider it a success. After all, compared to what I had been doing in my former life, or what I saw others achieving online, this seemed like nothing.

This is why we should never live life by comparison. Whether it's to our past or to other people, when we try to be as good as what we perceive to be the standard, we often find ourselves lacking. And that begins our downward spiral of beating ourselves up for not meeting benchmarks that often have nothing to do with our season or situation.

We start doubting ourselves and thinking there must be something wrong with us. In my case, I kept asking is it the message, or my marketing? Is it the *Loving on Me* name, or the positioning? Eventually, I thought, *Well, maybe people just need a break from my voice.* Lord knows I was tired of writing.

Posting with such frequency was wearing on me. I found myself struggling to find new topics and fresh ideas. So I decided to invite some friends to join me by sharing their stories. After all, this was supposed to be a movement. Surely that meant there should be more than one voice, right?

To my delight, the first series of guest posts were a smashing success. They ran as a lead in to Mother's Day. Seven women of various backgrounds and ages shared their perspective on being a mom while being "me." I loved how each piece came from a different perspective, challenging our thinking and encouraging us for the road ahead. This was the freshness the site needed, and the stats were booming to boot.

By midweek I was already planning my next series of guest posts when an unexpected guest appeared. It was the day when one of my dearest friends and biggest cheerleaders posted her guest blog. An incredible woman of faith with a lovely family and fantastic career, she had graciously agreed to write, and her friends were visiting the website in droves to read her post. It was the most successful day the website had ever experienced, and I was thrilled. But, I was also a little jealous.

Okay, a *lot* jealous. I mean, geez, I had been writing for months and nowhere near this many people came to read my posts. How come I couldn't get people to respond this way? Did my writing suck? God, why do you have me doing something that clearly other people are better at?

As you can see, in record time, I became completely irrational and ungrateful. But, unfortunately, that's what happens when the green-eyed monster comes for a visit. We quickly become consumed with envy, and instead of seeing things as they are, we fixate on how we perceive they should be, causing us to make bad decisions based on our warped view of reality.

Surprised that I was so petty? Yeah, I was too. If you had asked me if I was a jealous person, I would have said no without hesitation. I genuinely enjoy celebrating the success of others, and honestly can't recall another time in my life when I was so bent out of shape about being bested.

But even though I didn't know, or perhaps wasn't ready to admit it to myself, it's clear God knew. This was an area of my life that needed work before He could take me to the next level. You see, what I was feeling really wasn't about my friend. I wasn't unhappy that she got more attention. I was feeling insecure because I didn't think I got enough, that I didn't measure up in ways that mattered. I was still trying to be "enough."

Yep! The same issue I had been struggling with was threatening to stifle my growth yet again. It's funny how in life we can go three steps forward, then slide back two, and then over one. We want to move forward in a linear fashion, but sometimes it takes a lifetime to really conquer our challenges. And even then, conquering them often means we can control our response and bounce back quicker, not that we're ever fully released from the struggle.

It also means we have to learn to avoid our triggers and identify those things that are likely to throw us off track. For me, it was my ego. Even though God told me that *Loving on Me* was enough, I didn't quite believe it. My ego said it has to be bigger, more grandiose to be effective. And my insecurity over my season in life was constantly feeding me the message that I was not doing enough to "make it happen."

It's not a pretty picture, and I'm certainly not proud, but I also know I'm not alone. Many of us have allowed our egos to enslave us to achievement. We live and die by the dollars in our bank account, letters behind our name, and fans we have on social media. We sum up our success, not by the impact we make in the life of another, but by the number of others who acknowledge our work.

Trouble is, folks are fickle. What is celebrated one day is often criticized the next. As a result, we become like the proverbial hamster on a wheel, going round and round without really getting anywhere.

But if we want a more certain path for true and lasting success, we should focus our energy on pleasing God rather than garnering the praise of people. His desire is that we be triumphant from the inside out, with pure motivations at the core of what we do.

*The Lord doesn't see things the way you see them.
People judge by outward appearance, but the Lord
looks at the heart.*[5]

God is interested in our spiritual growth, not just our personal achievement. Does he want and expect us to be successful at what He's called us to do? Absolutely! But not always in the way we think, or according to our timeline, and certainly not with lingering issues in our life that will limit our ability to see the grander plan.

I'm grateful that God held me in place so I could see clearly areas of my life that still needed attention. I had to confess my mess, and ask God to forgive me and help me pull that junk up by the root, because a jealous spirit, driven by ego, would have caused me to miss the *more* God had in store for my journey.

You see, once I was no longer blinded by my own selfish need to be the popular one, I was able to put things in the right perspective. I saw that while I was busy worrying about how many views I could attract to the blog, and secretly trying to make sure I got the most, God was busy building a platform—one on which many women could help build a global movement, a caring community, and a business that I'm certain will expand far beyond what I can envision.

Isn't that something? Here I am trying to be writer extraordinaire, with thousands of people reading my work each month, and that wasn't even God's focus. He had a much richer plan, one that used my gifts as a builder to help lift up the lives of others in ways I could not have imagined.

I really begin to see this play out over the next several months, as I invited more and more women to share their stories. Eventually, we formed a group of featured writers, nearly a dozen

---

[5] 1 Samuel 16:7 NLT

women from every decade of life, who on a monthly basis shared insight and inspiration from their journey.

At first, I was still tracking the numbers, watching as web traffic continued to grow. But as time went on, I began to notice a trail of transformations. The more we transparently shared our trials and triumphs, the more confident we became. As writers, we seemed to be more in sync to the gentle whispers of the Spirit as we learned to quiet the chaos of our minds so we could hear the words we were to share. Concurrently, powerful life-changing shifts were happening, and I could only marvel at how God orchestrated such a dynamic experience. In just eighteen months ...

- four of us started new businesses;
- three of us changed careers;
- two of us went back to school;
- one of us wrote a book, and the one you're reading finally took shape.

Several of us also moved and got unexpected promotions, and all of us grew spiritually as our faith was stretched in new and unexpected ways. Our commitment to "be the me God created me to be"—and to share that with the world—unleashed the power of faith in action, and it was manifesting in a life of love and abundance.

Now, just imagine if I had let my little ego get in the way of God's big plans. I would have missed out on my own transformative experience, and the joy of celebrating His work in the lives of others—not just the writers, but in everyone they touched, because just like my leap of faith, theirs created ripples in the pond, and all around them lives were, and still are, changing for the better.

It occurs to me that this is how movements are born. This is how millions of lives can be touched, and we can transform our world—not by trying to do it all ourselves, but by seeing and serving the people God places before us, and encouraging them to be a part of serving others.

My desire to change the world led me to believe I had to do more to be more effective. But God says to passionately work in the field He has placed before us and patiently wait for Him to show us the next move. He is a force multiplier who can take our little and make it so much more.

I admit, I don't always get this right. I have to resist the urge to rush ahead and force my way down what I think is the right path for success. Occasionally, I still find myself looking at what others have achieved, and asking, "When, Lord? When will I get to speak again, to lead again, to be on an international stage sharing this important message? Don't you see how hard I'm trying? I'm ready!"

Yeah … I still have those days. Only now when I hear myself slipping into that mindset, I understand why I'm not ready. There's a part of my heart that still wants to be seen, and not really to serve according to His plan. God and I are working on that, and as I grow in grace, love, humility, and wisdom, I know that He will expand my territory.

There's a plan for your growth too. It begins with some gentle pruning in areas where you may be struggling. For you it may not be jealousy or ego. Maybe it's anger, resentment, bitterness, or selfishness. Perhaps it's pride, procrastination, or judgment. Could it be fear?

I don't know, but you do. It's apparent in those errant thoughts that run through your mind when you look or listen to others. It's what you think before you catch yourself and say now you know better than that. It's what is keeping you stuck, busy but not really making any progress. We want to believe it's a lack of opportunity, of direction, or perhaps even destiny. We sometimes think God is punishing us by not telling us what's next. But here is the truth:

The vision for our lives, the one we were destined for before we were born, emerges in direct proportion to our maturity to handle it.

Sometimes we need to grow up a bit before we're ready to go the next phase of our journey. I have come to the conclusion that while God created us whole and complete, our attitudes, beliefs, and perceptions are all still very much a work in progress. The great news is no matter where we're starting from, He is there and will guide us through.

As you think about what may need trimming in your own life, let the following be your personal prayer of peace and promise. There have been many days when I've had to read it and remind myself God knows me from the inside out—and He loves me anyhow. He's got a plan for my life, and even when I veer off track, He still keeps me right on time.

The same is true for you! Write the following passages in your journal. Memorize and meditate on them. Be at peace knowing the all-powerful God loves and cares for you. ❧

O Lord, you have examined my heart and know everything about me. You know when I sit down or stand up. You know my thoughts even when I'm far away. You see me when I travel and when I rest at home. You know everything I do. You know what I am going to say even before I say it, Lord. You go before me and follow me. You place your hand of blessing on my head. Such knowledge is too wonderful for me, too great for me to understand!

You made all the delicate, inner parts of my body and knit me together in my mother's womb. Thank you for making me so wonderfully complex! Your workmanship is marvelous—how well I know it. You watched me as I was being formed in utter seclusion, as I was woven together in the dark of the womb. You saw me before I was born. Every day of my life was recorded in your book. Every moment was laid out before a single day had passed. How precious are your thoughts about me, O God. They cannot be numbered! I can't even count them; they outnumber the grains of sand!

Search me, O God, and know my heart; test me and know my anxious thoughts. Point out anything in me that offends you, and lead me along the path of everlasting life.[6]

BOOKSHELF *boost*

If you're going through a tough transition and struggling to be patient as you grow, I recommend picking up a copy of *The Way of Transition: Embracing Life's Most Difficult Moments,* by William Bridges. It explains so much about what you're feeling, and tells you how to navigate the stages of transition.

You can find it at http://katrinamcghee.com/books/.

---

[6] Psalm 139:1–6, 13–18a, 23–24 NLT

I Am Expectant

I don't know where I'm going, but I know who's taking me.

O ne of the best gifts we can give ourselves is learning to celebrate progress. Doing so helps us stay happy and hopeful during the spring seasons of life, when we can see the buds of new beginning but we're not quite in full bloom. It also gives us a moment to stop and appreciate how far we've come and to express gratitude to the many people who've uplifted and inspired us along the way.

I used the first anniversary of *Loving on Me* for such an occasion. I wanted to have a small gathering to honor the thousands of women who were now in some way connected to the movement, and my friends at *Women that Soar* graciously offered to host it. This was especially sweet to me because Gina, the founder of WTS, was one of the first people to see and believe in the vision God had given me.

Just two months after I started *Loving on Me,* she held her annual gala and presented me with a *Women that Soar Emerging Entrepreneur Award,* an honor I didn't feel I yet deserved. In fact, I tried to talk her of out of selecting me as an honoree, but Gina saw things differently. She was sensitive to God's hand at work in my life and jumped on board to support by sowing seeds of expectancy—with words and action.

Many times I'd pick up the phone and it was Gina, calling to check on me and encourage me to stay on the path, even when my progress seemed painfully slow. What an incredible blessing it is to have people such as her in our lives, and to be such a person for those around us. Because I've learned **when women band together in passionate purpose, there is nothing we can't do**. Supporting others is a part of fulfilling our own purpose in life.

This is why, as we were planning the party, I made a decision to support the work of my friend Cheryl. *Loving on Me* hadn't yet made any money, but that didn't matter to me. I took funds from my consulting business and made a donation on behalf of the movement to Minnie's Food Pantry. Started in honor of Cheryl's mom Ms. Minnie, the pantry was just a few years old and already serving meals to thousands of families each month.

They were caring for people like me—in transition and in need of a hand. Sure, they may have had a different personal crisis than my own, but I believe everyone who experiences a life-interrupted moment shares a common bond, because we understand what it feels like to have our life upended, turned inside out, and spun around. Doesn't matter the cause, the effect is the same—a dizziness that leaves you lost, and for a time unable to find your way.

But I'm telling you, when God delivers you to the other side, you can't help but reach back and lend a hand. Gratitude is a powerful motivator for giving. And when we allow our gifts to be used in areas where God is already working, they become potent fertilizer for His field of plenty.

The theme for our party, *Celebrating What is and Yet to Be*, affirmed that belief, as we took a moment to highlight what we'd already accomplished and looked forward with sweet anticipation for what was yet to emerge. I invited all the writers who had graciously agreed to share their stories on the blog, as well as many others in the Dallas area who had helped us get started. It was important to me that we celebrate together so I could publicly express my gratitude to those who played an important role in my journey.

You know we often overlook this step, but people appreciate being appreciated. We want to know that what we do for others matters. But so often our society celebrates the spirit of independence rather than the beauty of interdependence. We revere people we believe do it on their own, or as we often say, "pull themselves up by their own bootstraps." Yet all of us know we were born naked and without a cent to our name. Were it not for God's grace, the kindness of people, and the care of angels, not a one of us would be here.

But pride in our hard work and achievements can fuel an "I did it on my own" mentality, causing us to overlook the generous spirit of those we take for granted. We forget that God works through us to take care of each other's needs, and for that we should be profoundly grateful, not just because it's the right thing to do, but because of the inherent benefits it brings to our own lives. Here's a little secret:

Embracing an attitude of gratitude leaves little
space for the spirit of lack to dwell in our life.

When we're truly thankful for what we have, we recognize it
as an overwhelming abundance from God, and we're confident
that it's enough for our journey. We also look at the future through
the lens of hope—expecting more is always in store.

We hold this expectation, not in a greedy, materialistic fashion,
but with a clear understanding that life is an ever-evolving journey.
Changes, even the painful ones, create crossroads, providing
decision points that reveal our next steps. And gratitude gives us
the courage to go forward, because if we understand what God
has done before, we can trust Him to carry us on.

Many of you can testify to what I'm saying. You were down
on your luck and had no idea how you'd make ends meet.
Unexpectedly, you got a gift in the mail to bridge the gap. Or
you lost a loved one and didn't think you could go on. But God
surrounded you with an army of angels and called them friends.
They carried you until you could stand on your own. Maybe you
were floundering, unsure of what to do next with your life. Then
suddenly God placed someone new in your path, inspiring you to
head in a previously unforeseen direction. Time and time again,
God surrounds us with the people and provision we need to be
successful in every season of life.

This is an incredible source of comfort, given the seasons
are always changing. We don't always get a clear sense of which
direction things are headed, but we can almost always sense an
impending shift. For months that had been happening to me as
I noticed subtle changes in my attachment to things and places.
One morning I woke up, looked around my house, and it seemed
too full. I felt a strong urge to get rid of all my extra "stuff."
The more I sold, donated, or discarded, the more I realized how

much I had been holding on to that I no longer needed. It was a cathartic experience, releasing many of the accouterments of my old life and making space for what lay ahead.

I also stopped purchasing new things. As much as possible, I used what I had and saved as much money as I could. I wasn't following a plan per se, but more so listening to the gentle nudging of the Spirit. Over and over again I heard the same message: Travel light and enjoy the journey. I couldn't let things weigh me down.

My spirit was getting restless, and I knew it would soon be time to go. To where was still a mystery, but once again, who was taking me there was clear. God was sending me in a new direction, and leaving no doubt that it was He who was charting my course.

Slowly He had been releasing me from everything tying me to Dallas. My cousin who had lived with me for a couple of years decided to get her own place. My son made the decision to go to graduate school out of state. And my livelihood was now possible from anyplace that had Internet access and a major airport.

All the signs were there, and I started praying for wisdom and discernment. I wanted to be ready, but not rush. For the first time in my life, I wanted to be completely open. Rather than giving God my choices, I wanted what He wanted for my life—however, whenever, whatever.

I talked to God about it for months with seemingly nothing changing. Then, two days before Thanksgiving, I woke up, and I knew. The spirit was telling me it was time to move to New York. There was no specific reason why, just a clear message that was the place, and the time was now.

I was so excited, although on paper, the decision to leave Dallas made no sense at all. First, it was the dead of winter—not the best time to sell my house or make a cross-country move north. Second, the cost of living would be two or three times higher. And third, I had no guaranteed income. That's right—none. All my consulting contracts were set to expire at the end of the year. If I stayed in Texas, I could live off my savings for quite a while. But in New York, it was going to last just long enough to unpack and find the grocery store.

I could list about a hundred more reasons why making the decision to go was a bad idea, but I only need one to tell you why it was the right choice for me. God said go. Go now, where I have told you. And I said okay, I'm with you.

Now, if you started reading the book at this chapter, I know this must seem kind of strange. In fact, you may think I'm a straight-up lunatic—hearing messages from God, making decisions that have no apparent logical basis, and doing it with excitement. Well, you're not alone. Many of my friends thought I was cuckoo too.

When I'd tell people I was moving to New York, the first question they'd asked was why. I'd say, "God said go, so I'm going." Imagine the looks I got when I said it and stopped talking. It's funny when I think about the dumbfounded expression on their faces. They weren't sure whether to congratulate me or try to have me committed. Who up and moves across the country without a good reason?

Good reasons, as they defined them, were a new job, new business opportunity, or a new boyfriend. Surely there was a reason other than surrendering to God's plan that would cause me to sell my house, all my furniture, my car, and just about everything else I owned to traipse across six states. Oh, and to a city where I barely knew anyone, and though I had visited many times, knew precious little about. Yeah, right ... "Katrina, are you sure you don't have a new boyfriend?"

That's the question I got the most, which was a little disappointing, because in talking to other women, I discovered that we will follow a man around the world, but so often won't make a move around the corner for ourselves, let alone be open and obedient to the urging of the Spirit. When it comes right down to it, we have a hard time letting "God and I" be enough.

Oh, but He is! Not only is He enough, He is everywhere and everything we need. We can be assured that when He puts things in motion, He does so with purpose and planning. All those excuses our minds conjure up for not being obedient to the promptings of the Spirit have already been handled. Our job is to say yes, do what we can, and watch with expectation as God goes to work.

The minute I said, "Okay, God I'm with you," things begin to domino into place. I had no particular timeline, but clearly God was working with a sense of urgency. Within thirty days I had found an apartment in New York, gotten a contract on my house in Dallas, and been contacted by two of my three clients to extend our agreement. Yippee! I was rocking and rolling, riding a high like you wouldn't believe ... right up until that contract fell through on the house.

It was the day before I was to sign the lease for my apartment, and suddenly I had a moment's hesitation. Wait a minute ... *Am I really supposed to be doing this?* I'm leaving everything I know, giving up what I already own, and moving halfway across the country—with no idea why, other than that God said so. Maybe I'm moving too fast. I should probably wait until I sell the house before heading out.

Suddenly, all those logical reasons my friends tried to persuade me with came rushing back. Perhaps they were right. Was I rushing when I should have been waiting?

Doubt sure is an insidious little devil. I've talked about it a lot in the book because I've struggled so often to overcome it. Even when I'm sure of something, one little detour or setback, and doubt rears its ugly head once again. The good news is I now recognize what it means—I've taken my focus off what God will do, and instead focused on what I think I can do.

He had already assured me He had a plan, so why was I about to let one minor holdup send me to the sidelines? Nope! Not this time. I was going to be obedient, immediately, not when I felt ready, but when He said it's time.

So I signed my lease, and a month later moved to New York. Believe me, it wasn't all smooth sailing. There were a lot of hiccups along the way, a lot of times when I had to just let go and grow with the flow, allowing God to mature me as He took my faith to new heights.

That's the key, you know: to take God at His word, truly trust Him, and anticipate the future with an air of expectancy. I know, sometimes it's hard to look at our present circumstances and remain hopeful about what's ahead. When things are tough or we're in the midst of change, it's difficult to see past the struggle. But it is possible, if we learn to focus on God's promises rather than ruminate on challenging conditions.

I was reminded of this principle a couple of weeks ago when my friend and I learned to paddle board. It's a water sport where you stand on what's basically an oversize surfboard with a fin on the bottom, and you use an oar to paddle across the water. Now, before we could stand up, we had to get used to the motion of the water. So the instructor had us wade out from shore and then slowly come to our knees on the board. For a while we stayed in that position, learning how to balance and paddle on both sides of the board.

But when we reached smoother waters, he came alongside us and taught us how to stand. He told us if we kept our eyes focused on the horizon, rather than looking down at the water, we'd be able to keep our balance. And after a bit of practice, we saw he was right. Once we got the hang of it, we sailed along.

However, there were moments when the wind would pick up, the waves would get really choppy, and it became more difficult to stand. I was tempted to go back down to my knees until I could regain a bit of my balance. But then it hit me —beneath me was water, I'm wearing a life jacket, and I can swim. What in the world was I worried about? Even if I lost my balance and fell into the water, I would still be okay.

That's what our hope in God gives us too—an assurance that we will be okay. If we learn to keep our focus on God's promises rather than our present circumstances, he'll help us stay balanced when facing turbulent times. We can enjoy riding the waves instead of worrying that we'll be swept away by the current. And when the winds of change pick up and we feel a little unsteady, we don't lose hope, because God is our life jacket! Even if we fall, there's already a plan in place to keep us safe in the end.

But now, if we choose to keep our eyes locked on our problems, we'll always be pessimistic about our prognosis, locked in the status quo as we search for our solution in what's causing us turmoil in the first place. Just like looking down at the water wouldn't allow me to move forward in a balanced fashion, focusing on our problems won't propel us beyond our temporary setbacks. All that does is depress us, keeping us from the glorious *more* God has in store.

The question is—how do you want to live? Do you want the hope His infinite wisdom and resources can provide? Or do you want the fear of failure that comes with trying to do it all on your own?

I hope you choose God's promises! They offer freedom, security and abundance. He says He will never leave you nor forsake you. His love never fails. He says He knew you before you were born and He has a plan for your good. He promises to be *with us always, even until the end of the world.*[7]

What He doesn't promise is that we won't have challenges, or face changes we don't enjoy. Those are in store for every one of us. But in the midst of it all, we can have hope. We can believe the gentle nudging of the Spirit, telling us to head in a different direction. We can be okay being obedient without having all the answers, and we can trust in His grander plan. And when doubt sets in, causing us to momentarily falter, all we have to do is refocus our eyes on Him.

Once when I was really struggling with this idea, my dad shared this Raymond Edman quote:

Never doubt in the dark what God told you in the light.

It's so easy to lose hope when everything doesn't go as planned. But I just want to encourage you to stay the course, and to approach each day expecting the best. It really is true that we get out of life exactly what we expect, as long as our expectations are rooted in God's promises and plans.

Don't let your circumstances lower your expectations. Instead, let your expectations encourage you to aim higher, believing that God's resources can catapult you into the realm of the unexplainable and unimaginable. If you're not sure you're hearing from God, or if you are struggling to believe what you heard is true, I encourage you to let this psalm be your prayer:

Show me the right path, O Lord; point out the road for me to follow. Lead me by your truth and teach

---

[7] Matthew 28:20 KJV

*me, for you are the God who saves me. All day long
I put my hope in you.*[8]

Decide today, right now, that you are going to update your expectations. Let your imagination run wild about what could be, if you had an opportunity. Then open your journal and write out your heart's desire as a letter to God. Ask Him to pour into you a fresh excitement about what He can do in and through your life. Then meet him on those pages daily, listening for his response, as He lovingly brings your desires in sync with your destiny.

Know this: No matter how many times you've messed up, stopped and started, or thrown up your hands and lost hope, if you are still here, there is still a purpose for your life. Ask God to help you live it, abundantly.

If you want more on the promises of God, I encourage you to read Joel Osteen's *I Declare: 31 Promises to Speak Over Your Life*. It's a month-long study on the blessings outlined in scripture and the promises God offers to us, His children.

It's a great way to stay encouraged and uplifted on the journey. Let's face it, every day we're not going to hit the mark. We're going to mess up, backslide, and make bad choices. But the stronger

---

[8] Psalm 25:4–5 NLT

our relationship with God, the easier it becomes to get up and start again.

Change the negative narrative in your head with a daily dose of *I Declare*. Visit http://katrinamcghee.com/books/ to pick up your copy.

I Am Faithful

God, I am all in with you!

L eaps of faith are great, but sometimes they come with a hard landing as our expectations take a beating from the harsh realities of our new normal. Mine certainly did when a blinding snowstorm hit New York two days after I arrived. Man, was it a brutal welcome. I had not experienced weather like that since I was a kid, and as the cold dragged on endlessly I thought I was going to freeze to death—which didn't seem that far-fetched given the Hudson River froze solid twice that season!

If I could have, I would have hibernated in my apartment until spring. But my eight-month old puppy Romulus had other ideas. Up every morning by 6 a.m., he was raring to go out and explore his new surroundings. This was his first experience with cold weather and snow, and unlike me, he loved it. His boundless energy and enthusiasm sent us out a lot those first few months, and to my surprise he adapted quickly to city living. Little things like riding the elevator and dog parks with no grass, which I thought might give him pause, turned out to be no problem at all. As long as he was with me, he was A-Okay.

I, on the other hand, took a bit longer to adjust. I trusted that I had made the right decision and that God had a master plan. But every once in a while when I was alone, unpacking boxes or wishing for someone to do fun things with, I would get lonely and really miss home.

Not the place, but the people. I longed for my family and close friends, and wished that obedience to God's plan—which I was still enthusiastic about—didn't require me to be quite so far away. My prayer was that whatever I had come to do wouldn't take long, or that I would quickly be able to expand my circle of friends, because life just wasn't as much fun without sharing it with the people I loved.

But God chose not to honor my request in the way I had hoped. Instead, over the next year I ended up spending a lot of time alone—me, Him, and of course, Romulus. I was disappointed at first, but after a while I understood that **God sometimes separates us from what we know best so we can get to know Him better**, especially in the area of faithfulness.

Not grand leaps of faith—those are fun and exciting, something new we're proud to share with others. I'm talking about faith around the everyday things, stuff we think we should be able to figure out on our own. I struggled with this in particular, as I was not always consistently on board with God's plan in areas I assumed would be governed by logic and roll out according to what I deemed a reasonable timetable. Things such as the sale of my house.

That initial flurry of activity where I had gotten a contract in mere days slowed considerably once I moved. After being in New York about five months, I'd only received a few purchase offers, all of which were way too low. I wanted to hold out as long as possible, waiting for just the right buyer, but I also wanted to be practical. Supporting two households for the long haul was not in my financial plan. The last thing I needed was to be stressed out about cash.

But the funny thing is, at the time I was doing all this worrying, I wasn't having any problems paying both sets of bills. My consulting company was thriving, and I was doing quite well. But still there was a voice inside my head that said maybe it's time to explore some other options. You don't want to deplete all your funds. Perhaps you should consider renting.

However, when I had said yes to God's plan, He had been clear that I needed to divest myself of all my stuff, including the house. I even knew that the new owner would be someone who was in transition who needed a place of peace, because the home I was selling was a healing house—a place where all who entered in could rest and be renewed.

I know that sounds odd, but it's true. When my realtor and I saw the house for the very first time, I knew at once, it was something special. There was a beauty and serenity that drew you in, and once inside, the house seemed to hug you into an intimate space.

The owner was home when we toured it, and as he showed us around, he asked me my story. I told him I had recently gotten a divorce, and it was time for a change. He looked a little shocked, but when he told me his story I understood why. "When I bought this house several years ago, I had just gotten divorced too. I can't explain it, but this house … it has a blessing attached to it. It helped me heal, and I think you'll be very happy here too."

Of course he could have been blowing smoke, but the sincerity of his voice rang true. And in the years that followed, I did indeed heal from the painful memories of my shattered happily-ever-after dreams. That's why, when it came time for me to leave, I felt strongly that I wasn't just selling the house. I was passing it on to the next person who needed healing.

My realtor, however, was much less sentimental. She thought I was putting way too much stock in the notion. She encouraged me to explore every potential buyer and option—including renting. And after another month with no solid leads, I finally acquiesced and reached out to one of the top property management firms in the city. They sent me all the paperwork, worked up the numbers, and gave me a couple of weeks to consider.

I went back and forth, trying to get comfortable with the whole notion of renting. But when it came down to it, I just couldn't leave the path God had laid out before me. Renting may have made sense financially, but it felt out of sync with my faith.

Have you ever had that experience? Some people call it wrestling with God, but I look at it more as fighting to stay faithful. It's when we start out on the right path, but things don't go according to a logical plan. At this point, we question the plan. We start looking for alternatives to the path—going down trails that lead to nowhere, only to find ourselves back where we started, having expended energy on worry that could have been applied elsewhere for the greater good.

My whole exercise in researching renting was like that for me. God had already told me to sell the house. I knew that was the right decision. But when things took longer than made sense—given the market, location, etc.—I started pursuing my own path. I pushed my faith in what God told me would happen to the back burner and depended on my own finite thinking, attempting to make logical sense out of what was clearly supernatural work.

How often we forget that at all times there are things happening beneath the surface and behind the scenes. What we see is never the whole story, and yet we so easily slip into making decisions as if this is all there is. But when we do, we cause ourselves unnecessary grief and worry. Just look at me! I worried about not being able to pay the bills, and never once had any indication that I was about to miss a beat. I was pre-worrying about something that wasn't even on the horizon, about to make decisions as if it were a foregone conclusion.

Many of you I speak with do the exact same thing. God has given you an opportunity to break out and try something new. You're excited and decide to go for it, but midway through, you run into a few bumps in the road. It jostles you a bit, and in no time your anxiety ratchets up because your mind has conjured up fears of what may be and might happen. Rather than stay the course, you head off in what looks like a safer direction.

We let our fears put us in bondage, even after God has set us free. But I am convinced we can do better. We must do better! If we want to experience life abundantly—filled with peace, purpose, and love overflowing, allowing us to be the "me" He created us to be—then we must practice walking in faith. We must be willing to take God at His word in all things, and we must face head on the fears that are weighing us down.

The question is, how? How do we stay faithful and release our fears, many of which have been with us for decades? By embracing one simple truth:

God is bigger than any problem we face.

When we embrace that as truth, the Spirit will give us the courage and power to move beyond our fears and stay focused on the path before us. Is it easy? Not at first. But when we learn to trust God consistently, with all things big and small, over time it gets easier.

What I've discovered is that **faith is like a muscle. The more you use it, the stronger it becomes**. It has to be exercised to be maintained and applied in every area of our life to really make a difference. That's what being faithful is all about—a steadfast approach to putting our trust in God.

It means that, come what may, you keep rolling with Him. Because guess what? He always knows the plan, and it's always the best approach—for you and for those around you. All we have to do is stay on the path—or in my case, get back on it.

Declining the proposal to rent the house delivered me from my own self-induced drama. I got back on track and told God I was all in with Him. Then I quit worrying about it, consciously changing my perspective and my conversation. Instead of being irritated about paying rent and a mortgage, I chose to thank God that I had the funds to do it. Instead of worrying about what was going to happen if I ran out of money, I chose to spend wisely. Rather than complaining to my family and friends about no contract, I'd just smile when asked and say, "It's going to sell."

I chose to believe that God was bigger than the problem I faced, and then I moved on down the path, doing what I could while I waited. Thirty days later, I had a contract. The buyer was a young woman who was in the process of getting a divorce. She was purchasing the place for her and her young daughter.

She wrote asking if I'd do an extended contract, waiting nearly three months to close so that she could finalize her divorce first. She said she and her daughter had taken one look at the house, and they both knew it was their new home. But they needed just a little extra time to get things in order before moving in. She needed grace, and I was grateful to be in the position to give it to her.

Blessing her blessed me. It brought tears to my eyes as I marveled at how God had orchestrated the circumstances. He intertwined two lives—both in transition—to see to each other's needs. The best part is, all it required was my faithfulness in order to bring it to fruition.

But I almost missed out, busy being busy, trying to make something happen when God already had the plan in motion. My worry didn't add anything to the equation except angst—causing me to waste time trying to put the plan on my timetable and creating issues where there were none. But when I came back to my right mind and got back on board with God, things worked out exactly as He said they would. Experience has shown me that when we allow Him to be a part of every detail of our lives, we can move forward with confidence.

Listen, I know for some of us this is really tough. We've had some bad breaks, and experience has taught us we are the only people we can depend on. We feel compelled to control every aspect of our existence, and when things don't work out as planned, we flip out, immediately going into fix-it mode.

I get it. The reason I didn't want to be stressed out about money is because I've experienced being unable to make ends meet, and, believe me, it is not fun. I've been broke, put out of my apartment, on government assistance, and at the mercy of friends and family for support. That is a season in my life I have no desire to repeat. So I do what I can to ensure I'm a good steward over what God blesses me to enjoy.

But I'm also realistic. As hard as we all try, there are a host of circumstances that we cannot control. One unexpected calamity can upset our whole life plan. Medical treatments can bankrupt us; the market can take a tumble, erasing our retirement account overnight; or we can suddenly lose our jobs, depleting the savings it took us years of sacrifice to build. Yes, all those things can happen. But we can never fully live if we operate from a base of fear that they will.

This is why one of the earlier lessons I shared was around the importance of not just getting over things from our past, but really taking the time to get complete. It was for this decision point right here. Because unless we heal from the hurts of the past, which are more painful than we care to acknowledge, they will continue to fester like raw unattended wounds, fueling our fear for the future. The freedom we need to move forward comes from releasing the guilt, shame, fears and defeat from our past. Otherwise we'll be good at starting down a new path, but our baggage will constantly drag us back into our old way of thinking.

But once we are free, a walk of faith is the key to unlock the *more* God has in store for our life. It is the answer to that yearning we feel in the depths of our soul. It's the reason you picked up this book and have read this far, because you are desperate to move beyond what has become your status quo.

I know some of you may be saying, "I really want to stay on the path but my faith is not as strong as yours." Well, guess what? Mine wasn't as strong either before this experience. Ironically, it's been this season of struggle that has given me strength. I've learned to talk to God about everything, to have a prayerful spirit, and seek His guidance as I go through the day. And it is that connection, spirit to Spirit, that gives me power to stand firm in the face of doubts, fears, and detours.

It is available to you too. My relationship with God is special, but not exclusive. He wants to pour into you as well, to give you the same stamina to stay faithful, and the power to fulfill your purpose. But He is not going to force it on you. You have to want it and prayerfully seek Him out in every area of your life. Don't hold back! Go all in with Him. Here's a prayer to get you started.

God I thank you for the desires you have given me and the passion to fulfill my purpose that comes from deep within. I have hopes and dreams, but I want more than anything to stay in sync with you. I want to get to know you and be renewed by your Spirit that lives within. Help me to stay faithful to the path you have placed before me. Don't let me be distracted, or defeated by doubt. Show me the way, Lord, in all things, and I will follow you. In Jesus name, Amen.

God hears you, and He understands. Now your next step is to change the words you are speaking to you. As God renews your spirit, you must also reframe your conversation, affirming your trust in His divine plan.

Giving voice to gratitude, expressing our expectations, and affirming our faith to those around us gives life to our hopes and dreams. It transforms our thinking and reframes our focus, so we are reminded of God's faithfulness to us, in turn encouraging us to be faithful to Him.

Try it today in the pages of your journal. Challenge yourself to write one page of gratitude, filled with all the good God has done. On the next page, talk to God about what you anticipate Him doing in the future. Don't be shy. He knows the desires of your heart anyway, so go ahead and express them honestly. Finally, make your last page a statement of faith. Declare your trust in Him, and commit to being faithful, come what may.

Remember, intentions and expectations are a great start, but it is faithfulness that will allow you to walk into your destiny. If you want the *more* God has in store for you, stay faithful to Him. ❥

BOOKSHELF *boost*

If you need help jumpstarting your walk of faith, I recommend picking up a copy of *Greater*, by Steven Furtick. In it he gives practical advice on how to dream bigger, start smaller, and ignite God's vision for your life.

It includes the powerful story of Elisha receiving God's call and "burning the plow," indicating he would never go back to his life as a farmer. So many times when I've thought about going back to my "safe" way of living, this passage has encouraged me to stay the course.

Find a copy here: http://katrinamcghee.com/books/.

Hope it blesses you!

LESSON TWELVE

I Am Unstoppable

All you have to do is stay focused, and keep it simple.

With God, all things are possible. Fully embracing this truth prepares us to move beyond the land of the ordinary into the realm of the extraordinary. It expands our vision so that it is no longer limited by what we can see. Instead, our hopes and dreams are based on what we believe. And when we believe God loves us, values our life, and has a plan for our future that is beyond what we can imagine, we begin to approach this business of living from a different perspective.

Our barometer for success changes, and we feel free to live out our soul's purpose. In fact, this becomes our only goal. All those things we thought we had to do or needed to achieve take a back seat to the growth and maturation process that brings us ever closer to our Creator and to our divine purpose.

As a result, we become much more sensitive to the Spirit's leading, and we learn to embrace with enthusiasm the unexpected twists and turns of our journeys. You can expect quite a lot of these when you ask God to show you His *more* for your life, partly because we have yet to understand how truly resting in Him is what releases us from our own limited perspective.

By the end of *Loving on Me's* second year, I was finally starting to learn this lesson. It had been an amazing season of growth and exploration. Unforeseen opportunities such as the launch of our online television show propelled us to new heights, greatly increasing our network of friends. Our family of featured writers also expanded, and just in time for the holidays, we finally launched our online store, featuring products that added affirmations to everyday life.

Things were clicking on all cylinders, and I could see the vision God had given me beginning to emerge. But I was also a little tired. Launching so many things at one time, along with running the consulting company, had taken a lot out of me. It had also taken my focus off completing the book, something I knew God was calling me to do.

As the end of the year approached, I once again got still to seek God's counsel. The message I kept hearing over and over was *slow down and keep it simple.* Focus on what's in front of you. If you do that well, the rest will follow.

So I said, "Okay God, I hear you. You know the desires of my heart, and, ultimately, what it is I was created to achieve. So rather than setting new goals or challenging myself to expand, I'm just going to work on whatever you place in front of me and try my best to do so with excellence. I'm not even going to put pressure on myself to finish the book. Instead I'm going to wake up every day and ask what would you like me to do, and whatever you say, I'll do. For the next twelve months my only goal is to please you."

Let me tell you, this was a radical approach for me! I've been a goal-setter my entire life. So this notion of winging it with God felt a little like an odd social experiment, and I had no idea how it was going to work out. I mean, how was I to track progress without benchmarks? And when would I know if God was pleased?

To be honest, I didn't expect to get much done. I figured I'd meander through the year, ending at pretty much the same place I began. Maybe this was God's way of giving me a break, allowing me to catch my breath before another busy stretch of road ahead. But I didn't worry about it. By now, I'd learned to trust Him. We had an intimate relationship, and whatever He had planned was for my good.

So my year of trying to please God begins and two things immediately happened. First, the team I assembled for managing *Loving on Me* began to part ways. One person got a job, another had major surgery, and yet another moved out of the country. Shortly after, some of the featured writers began to fade away too, causing a downward spiral in the number of people we were reaching each month. It seemed that, as hard as we'd worked to move forward, I was now going to have to take a step back and rebuild.

The second thing that happened was my consulting company's profits exploded, nearly doubling the previous year's revenue without increasing the number of clients. It felt like God had opened up the windows of heaven and poured out a blessing, one that, in all honesty, if I were Him, I'm not sure I would have decided I was worthy to receive. You see, the truth was I didn't want to do more consulting. I still wanted what I wanted, which was to be speaking more about *Loving on Me*. Consulting was fine, but it was building someone else's brand. I wanted to build my own.

I know some of you want to slap me upside the head. "Ungrateful little snot! Here she is able to successfully work at her own business, and still not satisfied."

Well, you're right. It was ridiculous, and I needed an attitude adjustment quick. But let me ask you a question ... are you content with what God has given you? How many times have you begged Him for something, received it in unanticipated packaging, and then turned up your nose at it?

Let's see ... could it be the spouse you prayed for but now, living together, find has some habits that get on your last nerve? Or perhaps it's that job you wanted so badly, but it turns out not to be exactly what you had planned? Sure, your spouse and job are blessings, but because they are so far from what you thought you wanted, it's easy to end up discontented.

Such was the scenario I was facing. The more time I spent consulting, the less time I had to build *Loving on Me*, which in my mind should have been my priority. That was my God-work, helping people be who they were created to be, to accept themselves as they are, and to know that they're enough. How could consulting be more important than that?

Well, God had quite a surprise for me! Because I had committed to work on what He placed before me, I put my all into consulting, and after a couple of months an amazing thing happened. I fell in *love* with it. Especially the training courses.

Sales, personal branding, and business development—they all included an element of helping people find and tap into their God-given natural gifts and abilities, identifying who they were created to be and for what purpose. Encouraging them to operate from this base of strength, rather than expending all their energy on fixing their weaknesses, naturally led them down a path that was custom designed for their success. And the bonus was that when I looked at their faces, I knew this unconventional approach was working for them. I could see their inner light beginning to shine brighter, and I felt mine doing the same.

How ironic that the very thing I was asking God for, I already had, but I didn't recognize it. I had relegated the core message of *Loving on Me* to the company I had created. But God had designed it as the central theme of my life. I, who had been a hot mess just a few short years before, was now being used by Him to share this powerful message of love and acceptance with the world. Through the consulting company, He was giving me the opportunity to teach it to people who were in a position to share it with others—leaders and sales professionals whose job it was to speak to people.

I'm so excited I want to get up and run around the room. Ain't God good? Here I was begging Him for more time to work on a blog that, at that point, was barely getting any traffic, so that I could launch a motivational speaking career that would, quite possibly, pay me less than training but have me traveling ten times more. Thank goodness He did not give me what I thought I wanted, but instead showered me with what He knew I needed.

And praise be I had the courage to take Him at His word and walk the path less traveled. I am certain it's because I took the time to build a relationship with our God who lives, and loves us so much He is interested in every facet of our lives. Were it not for those first eleven lessons I outlined in this book, I would have never gotten to this place of peace, joy, and life abundant. I would not have been able to go the year without a plan, or hidden agenda, or something to make sure if my social experiment didn't work I had a fallback.

But since I did, I had the amazing experience of kicking the ladder of success to the side and learning how to soar. God allowed me to make a quantum leap, reaching a higher plane that I had no idea existed. This is the extraordinary life He promised. But three years ago I could never have imagined it was only accessible through a deeper relationship with Him. Just like you, all I knew was there had to be more than what I'd had before.

Fortunately, my search lead me to reconcile the disparate parts of myself back to Him. And it is that process that has set me free. Now I can say with assurance **I am unstoppable**. Not because I am Superwoman—I've tried that, and I've decided to give up the cape for good. Nor am I the smartest girl in the room—tried that too and ran right into the brick wall of my own limitations.

Instead **I am a masterpiece**, a one-of-a-kind unique design. I am made in God's image, created for His purpose, and endowed with the gifts I need to fulfill my divine assignment. As Pierre Teilhard de Chardin said, I am "a spiritual being having a human experience," madly in love with the God that makes all things possible.

Now I don't measure success by what I achieve, but how I choose to live. Am I becoming more of who He created me to be? Am I obeying the whispers of the Spirit? Am I letting the light of His love shine through? Those are the hallmarks of what I consider a successful life. And I find when I focus my energy there, God orchestrates every other area of my life for his glory and my good.

And by "good" I'm not just referring to financial success. I know some of you reading this might think my sense of confidence comes from the consulting company's profitability, that I merely parlayed my career expertise into a successful business and can afford to carry this love message on the side, having secured a steady stream of business. But I'm going to tell you a little secret.

I have never pursued a consulting client. Not one. They have all been handpicked by God and brought to me as my place to serve in this season. He has supplied all of my needs, and I operate in total dependence on Him. It's an uncommon life, but one that is free from worry. Although I never know who I'll be working with next, I'm always certain who I'm working for, and He is the God that owns it all.

I pray you experience the same kind of peace in your own life, the kind only He can give, that surpasses all human understanding. Yours may have nothing to do with business or finances, but I can assure you that whatever you need, He can provide. But you have a role to play too, and that's total surrender and obedience to Him. If you're willing to give God your all, He'll give you everything you need, and so much more.

However, if you've read this entire book, done the journaling, and are still unsure how to access the *more* God has in store for you, I'm going to suggest you do four things:

1. **Reevaluate your relationship with God.** We can't trust someone we don't know, or put our faith in His promises if we don't believe in Him. So go back and read Lesson 3 again, ensuring you're on solid ground before you try to walk further down the path.

2. **Check your baggage.** Next to not having a relationship with God, the number one reason we cannot move beyond our comfort zone is that we won't let go of the past. Listen, there is no way I could've made a quantum leap while holding on to my guilt and shame, and you can't either. Whatever is weighing you down, take the time to get complete so you can let it go. You'll never reach higher ground with the weight of the world on your back.

3. **Listen to the Spirit.** The Holy Spirit doesn't yell, but there's no need when we can hear the whispers quite clearly. The key is to listen with an open heart, and try our best to obey. Amazingly, I find that when we do, we

get more direction. I can't say I always understand it at the moment it's given, but I trust it's for my good. The Spirit has a word for you too. Get still and listen so you don't miss your instructions.

4. **Work where you are planted.** The final reason we struggle with moving beyond the status quo into the realm of the extraordinary is because we refuse to bloom where we're planted. We haven't let go of the preconceived notion of how our paths should lay out, and with what speed we should move forward. But if you want life abundantly, you have to be willing to start with what you have, where you are planted. Don't let what you think should be keep you from taking what is and co-creating with God what could be.

There's no doubt about it—it takes hard work to live a life beyond what you can hope or imagine. But it is accessible to all of us, if we believe. Just stick with it until you experience your moment of transcendence, and then watch God put the whole of the universe in motion to support your success.

Opportunities you didn't even know were possible will suddenly appear. Your job will be to stay alert and ready so you can see, recognize, and seize them as they pass by. To do so takes confidence, courage, and perseverance.

Our confidence is fueled by faith so that our vision goes far beyond our sight. It allows us to have hope and dream big, based on the desires God has placed in our hearts. Here's how it's described in Scripture.

Faith is the confidence that what we hope for will actually happen; it gives us assurance about things we cannot see.[9]

When we have confidence, we can be courageous, boldly putting our faith in action. A lot of us assume we don't have enough courage to move forward because we're afraid, but that's not true. **True courage is not the absence of fear. It is the will to do in the midst of our doubt.** This is why we have to be careful not to fall into the trap of just trusting ourselves. In order to face our fears and move forward anyhow, we need to be powered by a source much bigger than ourselves.

Finally, we need perseverance for when we get weary and worn, when we come up against roadblocks and obstacles, naysayers and fools. There will be a hundred things that will block our path, but with perseverance we will not be defeated. When we get discouraged, I want you to remember this:

I can do all things through Christ who strengthens me.[10]

Confidence + Courage + Perseverance = Success. Together they form our core of steel, so that when the winds of change blow, we can stand strong. And in order to enjoy the journey, we must couple those with an attitude of gratitude.

There is no better elixir for a sweet life than gratitude. It's the quickest way I know to change our outlook when we can't yet change our circumstances. No matter how tough life gets, there is always something for which we can be grateful. And the best part is that gratitude reciprocates. The more grateful we are, the more life gives us to be grateful about. Practice gratitude as a way

---

[9] Hebrews 11:1 NLT
[10] Philippians 4:13 BSB

of life. Don't be like I was above—so set on what I thought I wanted, I almost missed out on the joy of what I had. Let's be grateful for our blessings, even when they appear in unexpected packages. In fact, I've learned to relish those the most—knowing God is revealing more than what I had imagined.

Finally, let's power up by letting love lead the way. It's the strongest force in the universe, and it is always available, ready to be unleashed in our life. There's a never-ending well within each of us, which is constantly being renewed by the Spirit who helps us fulfill what Christ said is the most important commandment:

> *You must love the Lord your God with all of your heart, all your soul and all your mind. This is the greatest commandment. A second is equally important: Love your neighbor as yourself.*[11]

We were made for a love relationship with God, and there will never be anything that can take its place. We can try to substitute material possessions, accolades, and achievements, but they will never be enough. Until we accept and return God's love, there will always be a hole in our hearts that nothing else will fill.

We will also never be able to fully embrace the second commandment to love our neighbors as ourselves. I know a lot of us struggle with what exactly this means. Do we have to love ourselves first? Can we love others without loving ourselves? Isn't it selfish to love you? I've spent a lot of time reading various theologians' perspective on the issue. Truth is, many of them contradict, and I fear we may have intellectualized the discussion so much we've missed the basic point.

We are commanded to love God, and to love our neighbor as ourselves. It is mentioned nine times in the Bible, exactly that

---

[11] Matthew 22:37 NLT

way. God could have just said, "Love your neighbor," and never mentioned ourselves. But he didn't. I believe that's because when we learn to love and accept ourselves as He created us, and for the purpose for which we were designed, it becomes infinitely easier to offer the same to others.

So let's not get caught up on which one to do first. Let's just do it! Love God with everything you've got, love your neighbors liberally, and love yourself, unapologetically. Let His unlimited love for you be how you strive to love others, allowing it to overflow into the lives of those around you, by serving and meeting the needs of those you see. Doing so will unleash the greatest power in the universe, propelling us all ever closer to fulfilling our destiny.

As we close out this last lesson, I want you to take a moment and love on you. So pull out your journal, settle down with a hot cup of coffee or tea, and write a love note to you. Start by celebrating the wonderful creation you are, your unique gifts, and the many ways God has allowed them to be used to enhance the lives of others. Then I want you to lovingly identify areas where God is still bringing out the best in you. Don't judge, just observe, so you can be more aware of the gentle whispers of the Spirit redirecting your course in those areas.

Finally, I want you to get a Post-It note and write down the five ingredients to an unstoppable life: Confidence, courage, perseverance, gratitude, and love. Post it somewhere prominent, so you can see it every day. If you learn to make these a part of your everyday life, you will live beyond what you can hope or imagine, and experience life abundantly. ♥

BOOKSHELF *boost*

I recently read *The Alchemist*, the story of a shepherd boy named Santiago who goes in search of his Personal Legend, or as we would say, his destiny. The tale is full of twists and turns that eventually lead him to discover more about God, himself, and the infinite possibilities in the world around him.

If you need a broader perspective of what it really means to go get your *more*, I recommend picking up a copy. Paulo Coelho does a magnificent job of creating a world in which we all can believe and achieve greatness, according to our divine plan.

Here is a link: http://katrinamcghee.com/books/.

THE ROAD AHEAD

Although this leg of our journey is coming to a close, this too is a place of new beginnings. That's how life works. We struggle, toil, and persevere, until we reach what we think is the end, only to find there is *always* more in store. For me, it means the book is finished, but I'm just getting started. God has big plans, and I can feel myself as the phoenix rising, just about ready to take flight.

I firmly believe this message of courageously being who we were created to be has the power to change your life too. That's why at www.lovingonme.com you'll find a variety of resources all designed to help you successfully step out of your comfort zone. What I'm most excited about is our free video learning series, created to help you put the lessons you've just read about immediately into action in your life. There's also a discussion guide for book clubs and study groups, so you and a small group of friends can take this walk of faith together.

I'm so grateful God has given me the privilege of sharing what I have learned with you. My prayer is that reading my story will inspire and ignite you to confidently go on your own adventure with Him. The question is, are you ready to commit? Are you willing to explore the *more* God has in store for you? Now that you've seen the transformative power of His work in my life, will you surrender and allow Him to do the same for you?

I sure hope so! We're all on a different path, but there are some universal truths to guide us. I tried to shine a light on them as we've walked together, but it's up to you to do the work. You must develop your own relationship with God, and be obedient to the whispers of the Spirit. You must seek His direction, and wait patiently for His response. And you must accept His love, along with the promises He has already given. These will guide you along your journey to the *more* he has in store for your life.

I can't wait to cheer you on and celebrate your success! If you sign up for our newsletter, you can get ongoing support from more of our *Loving on Me* tribe, along with reading stories of others who are boldly walking in faith. For daily inspiration you can connect with us socially on Facebook, Twitter, and Instagram @ iamlovingonme. We'll do our best to shower you with love and encouragement along the way.

I thank God often for taking my mess and turning it into a message. I know He can do the same for you. Regardless of where you are on your journey, you can make the choice not to spend another second stuck in status quo living. So go ahead, trust God, and go get your *more*!

I'll see you on down the road … in the realm of the extraordinary. Hugs and Love . ❤

ABOUT THE AUTHOR

Katrina McGhee is a woman of faith who isn't afraid to put it into action. As an advocate, entrepreneur, and non-profit professional, she's dedicated her life to improving the health and well-being of women and children around the world. Today she's also taken on a new role—a revolutionary passionate about unleashing the transformative power of God's love in our lives.

In 2012, she birthed *Loving on Me*, a global movement encouraging women to let go of the status quo and become more of the "me" God created them to be. Her bold vision is a tribe of sisters radically changing the way we view and value ourselves and each other. She's on a mission to inspire us to live life abundantly, and she's just crazy enough to believe that, with God's help, she can get it done.

Katrina currently lives in New York City, and is the proud mom of an adult son, Brandon, and a crazy puppy, Romulus.

For a special video message from Katrina, her speaking schedule and recent blogs visit www.KatrinaMcGhee.com.